UNDERSTANDING
GOD'S SUBTLE WORK AM

W;)NKS
from
SCRIPTURE

CHRIS PALMER

WHITAKER
HOUSE

WINKS FROM SCRIPTURE
Understanding God's Subtle Work Among Us

www.chrispalmer.me
www.instagram.com/chrispalmer

ISBN: 978-1-64123-846-5
eBook ISBN: 978-1-64123-847-2
Printed in the United States of America
© 2022 by Chris Palmer

Whitaker House
1030 Hunt Valley Circle
New Kensington, PA 15068
www.whitakerhouse.com

Library of Congress Cataloging-in-Publication Data (Pending)

1 2 3 4 5 6 7 8 9 10 11 **Ⱳ** 29 28 27 26 25 24 23 22

DEDICATION

This book is dedicated to those who could use a wink.

CONTENTS

PREFACE: THE BIRD AND THE WINK

It was a Saturday morning in 2005 in Minneapolis, Minnesota. The skies were clear, and the sun-dried leaves rustled along the concrete as I walked up Ninth Street. I meditated on Mark 16, which I had just finished reading.

I was a junior in college, headed for Target. Another exciting Saturday.

I had a funny thought around verse 15: *"Proclaim the gospel to the whole creation."* I chuckled, thinking, *Ha, I bet someone thinks this means preaching to animals.* I laughed and went into the superstore.

After I finished browsing, I headed back to my dorm, going down Ninth Street. I was feeling at peace, alone with my own thoughts. Suddenly, I was interrupted by a pigeon in distress, flapping its wings in the middle of the street. It was obvious this poor creature could not fly, having been injured in some catastrophic bird accident. I'm an animal lover, the kind of guy who occasionally enjoys going to the zoo. Animals have feelings, too, do they not? I didn't want to see this bird get smooshed flat by an oncoming car. Not on my watch.

Anxious drivers waited for the light to turn green. In seconds, they would be on top of the bird. I realized, *If I don't act, this pigeon won't be home for supper.* I dashed into the street, clutched the fowl to my chest, and dashed heroically back to the sidewalk, all in slow motion. I think I might have heard John Williams playing something in the background. I rescued a bird! Someone call the Humane Society and nominate me for an award for my lionheartedness!

Then, it dawned on me: now what? What is one supposed to do with a bird in the middle of a metropolis? Where could I put it? Cities are dangerous places, especially for an injured creature. Manholes can swallow you into the dark abyss, jackhammers can pound you into salt, and garbage trucks with claws can toss you into a heap made of waste.

People were staring at me awkwardly. I started to think this was a bad idea.

The college was around five blocks away, so I anticipated the longest, most self-conscious walk of my life. Then, I noticed my saving grace—an Episcopal church with a garden! I thought, *This will do splendidly. He can recoup in here.*

To my thinking, the garden was comparable to a rehabilitation center. The bird could take a few days off and then get back to business. I didn't consider that he had no food or water and would probably find his way back into traffic. But it wouldn't have mattered had I thought of it. I had already done my part. The hero needed to get back to campus.

I wonder what's going happen to this little guy, I thought. I knew I would never know.

Or would I?

That evening, I was walking into the cafeteria. Well, more like strutting. Casually, my friend Becky said, "Chris. You want to hear a weird story?"

(Why she even told *me* this story still baffles me. We weren't that chummy.)

"Yeah, why not?" I said. I love a good story.

"So, I am walking up Ninth Street today, and I am passing this Episcopal church," Becky began.

My eyes got as big as watermelons. I thought I was dreaming—either that or she was playing some kind of oddball joke on me. *Did I wake up this morning in the Twilight Zone?*

"I notice there's this little pigeon in the garden there," Becky said. "Have you ever seen that garden? Anyway, this pigeon is hurt. It can't fly. And it's got its poor little self all wrapped up in the cold iron fence that surrounds the garden. The poor thing was down on its luck. I felt I had to do something. So, I grabbed it! I clutched it to my breast. And I started walking up Ninth Street with it."

This was definitely the Twilight Zone.

"I got a few yards, and suddenly a car slams on its brakes. The window rolls down. It just so happens it was a University of Minnesota student. And here's the oddest part: she's studying to be a veterinarian!"

The Twilight Zone theme song thumped in my head.

"She tells me to hop in. She can help the bird; she can fix the little guy. We drive down Ninth Street and head to the university pet clinic. And guess what? They're repairing the bird's wing as we speak. Soon, it will be ready to fly again!"

I nearly fainted.

To this day, Becky does not believe that I got the pigeon out of the street and placed it in the garden. I spent two years trying to convince her, and she still wouldn't believe me. She *still* thinks I'm joking. Well, I'm not. That's precisely what happened that day. I have used this story in sermons for the last twenty years. I've even had other preachers take this story and tell it in their own way.

Great story, no? I've told it enough times to know what you are wondering right now. It's the same thing everyone always asks me.

"What does it mean?"

Thought you'd never ask. Allow me to lay it on you. Are you ready?

I don't know. No clue.

The more I think about that bird and the seemingly random way people stepped in to rescue it, the more mysterious it all becomes.

Oh, sure, you can go right to Matthew 6:26 and say, "See, God watches over the birds of the air. How much more does He watch over you and me!" Yeah, I've used this story to illustrate that. I have even told this story at a funeral. The organist went into a full-blown rendition of "His Eye Is on the Sparrow" in C sharp. People were encouraged and blessed.

But I was left unsatisfied. While the story can illustrate that God's eye is on the sparrow that cannot be the only meaning. Explaining it that way, and that way alone, falls short. Way short. It's truncated. Hackneyed. Oversimplified. And dare I say it's a cliché? All I know is that what happened that day with the pigeon meant that God does indeed watch over little birds...but *also* a whole lot more.

This reminds me of the apple tree that used to be behind my grandma's house. My brother and I used to shake it until it gave up its goods. No matter how often we came back, the tree always had something more to give. You just had to know how to shake it.

I'll take a moment to shake down my story from an outside perspective. Now, I realize it is *my* story, but I promise to be objective. To shake it, I want to look at it from two perspectives: the story itself, the actual details as I told them, and a few narrative features—those elements that make a story a story.

We begin with the actual details of the narrative, which are eerie, to say the least:

1. I was pondering the idea of preaching to all creation and humorously considered preaching to animals just moments before I stepped in to save a bird's life.

2. I placed the bird in a garden. Becky passed the same garden and noticed the same bird.

3. A car stopped right after Becky picked up the bird.

4. The car's driver was a veterinary student at the University of Minnesota who could rehabilitate the bird.

5. Becky randomly told me this story. If she hadn't, none of this would ever have been understood.

What is the probability of all this synchronicity?

Let's consider a few of the narrative features—the elements that make a story a story. Might these tell us more than the raw details?

1. Possible symbolism:

   a. A bird: not just any bird, but a pigeon—a dirty, insignificant pigeon.

   b. A garden: not just any garden, but a lush garden fortified by a fence and encompassing a house of worship in a raucous metropolis.

   c. The movement along Ninth Street: the bird begins in the street. Chris takes it *down* Ninth Street. Becky finds the bird and takes it back *up* Ninth Street. The car stops with the mystery driver and takes it back *down* Ninth Street. The movement is up and down the same street.

   d. Students: those involved in helping the bird were *all* university students.

e. Cars: cars were expected to be the bird's demise, yet it was a car that came to the rescue.

2. Characters:

a. Chris, the main character, is contemplative, smug, self-conscious, worried about how others see him, limited in how far his compassion will go (as proven by his dumping the bird the first chance he got), overly proud of himself for saving the bird, and disappointed that Becky doesn't believe he put the bird in the garden.

b. Becky is from the same Bible school as Chris. She's compassionate toward the bird and willing to get in the car with a stranger for its sake. Chris thought he had already done more than enough, but Becky goes the distance, all the way to the vet. She rejoices over the bird's well-being instead of exalting herself as a hero, as Chris did.

c. The nameless veterinary student in the car is from a public university. Beyond that, she's a mystery. We aren't sure where she came from or where she was planning to go. She enters the story and exits as quickly as she enters. We know little about her other than she is concerned for the pigeon and will interrupt her day for its sake.

d. The bird: innocent and helpless. We don't know how it got injured. It seems oblivious to anything happening to it. It doesn't seem to recognize foe from friend.

When we consider the details of the story and examine the narrative features, it looks like a lot more could emerge beyond, "His eye is on the sparrow, and I know He watches me."

We could go on shaking this story using other narrative features, but by now, you get the point. Looking at it through a few of the story elements, you can see that it can't be put into a nice little bundle of compacted meaning, saying it connotes *only this*.

That's why a truncated explanation of my story is unsatisfying. On one hand, yes, His eye *is* on the sparrow. But what about the garden symbolism, especially a garden within an unforgiving metropolis? How about three students who pulled this off? Or the characters' movements up and down Ninth Street? Or a student from a secular university appearing to have more compassion than me, a student from a Bible school?

Trying to determine one meaning behind this has left me exhausted. I've come to realize something in these nearly two decades: I don't need to know the totality of its significance. The mystery of it makes it a tree that keeps on giving. This is the power of story.

Biblical stories are *loaded* with mystery. That mystery keeps us asking questions about the story's details. In doing so, little ironies and nuances emerge that we hadn't seen before. This is God winking at us, letting us know He's there, guiding our lives.

Never disrespect yourself for uncertainty when you're reading a story, particularly in Scripture. Expect the uncertainty to be a tree that yields ever more fruitful takeaways as time goes by.

In this book, we will pursue New Testament stories using their details and the narrative features employed by the writers. We'll examine the ironies, the absurdities, and the elements in the story that give us added meaning beyond the obvious.

These subtle narratives—these *winks*—yield unforeseen lessons and have the effect of a punchline. They surprise us. They make us question what we thought we knew. The joke is on us for not seeing them to begin with.

But they tell us that God is here: He's at work, and He's in control. As a result, we wonder what else we haven't seen in the story. What else don't we know? What else is there to look for in a story we once thought we had figured out? It is this uncertainty that keeps us searching, pondering, and probing the text to discover more.

Catholic theologian G. K. Chesterton would encourage this. While Chesterton believed that Christianity answers life's questions, he also believed that Christianity is mysterious, and we are to question that mystery. Doing this keeps us thinking and searching, which is the way it should be. Chesterton wrote:

> As long as you have mystery, you have health; when you destroy mystery, you create morbidity. The ordinary man has always been sane because the ordinary man has always been a mystic. He has permitted the twilight...The morbid logician seeks to make everything lucid and succeeds in making everything mysterious. The mystic allows one thing to be mysterious, and everything else becomes lucid."[1]

When we allow the text to be a mystery, we keep coming to the text with our questions. And every now and again, the text will wink with added meaning, reminding us once again that God may be doing ten thousand things at any given moment, while we in our *certainty* are only aware of a few.

---

1. G. K. Chesterton, *Orthodoxy* (New Kensington, PA: Whitaker House, 2013), 25–26.

ACKNOWLEDGMENTS

By now, I've been writing long enough to be acquainted with myself in the writing process. My moods sway back and forth like lovers locked in a ballroom dance. A good day of writing can be followed by five days of no creativity and doubt as to whether I know the English language, followed by a short temper, irritability, and losing interest in my personal life. I get forgetful, too. I'll leave the house without my wallet, forget to return phone calls, and wind up at the store without remembering why I'm there. Those who love me have learned to be patient with me. And that takes *a lot* of patience, let me tell you. So here I'd like to acknowledge my family. Thanks for putting up with "Chris, the moody writer."

Next, I'd like to tip my hat to my influencers—those who have helped to shape my thinking and approach to the biblical text. Prior to knowing John Christopher Thomas, my Ph.D. advisor, I thought about Scripture only from a historical or grammatical standpoint. This meant looking at the history, culture, and syntax of the biblical writers—the world behind the text, as it's called in hermeneutics. Yet, in addition to this, Chris challenged me to think about the world inside the text—the narrative features such as plot, characters, setting, structure, dialogue, and sequencing. This led me to the writings of Jeannine K. Brown, James L. Resseguie, Mark Allan Powell, and others with a love for narrative criticism. *Winks from Scripture* came about as the result of reading and rereading their work.

I'd also like to thank Moody Bible Institute, where I taught Greek III, New Testament Survey, Old Testament Survey, and some other practical courses on preaching and intercultural ministry while writing this book. These classes allowed me to use some of my work in the classroom, explore my thinking, and glean ideas from students.

I can't forget Theos University. I spent a lot of time with the manuscript at Theos U in Palm Desert, California. Working with the Theos team gave me a chance to explore creative ways to communicate Christ-centered theology, which helped to shape *Winks*.

Thanks also to the amazing team at Whitaker House, especially Peg Fallon. And special thanks to Luana Minutella, whose feedback I always appreciate.

Last, I'd like to thank Mary Achor. I can't believe it's been a decade since I started working with her. She is the *subtle* reason I love to write.

It takes a village to write a book. And I'm thankful for the little village that has contributed to *Winks from Scripture*.

INTRODUCTION:
A WORD ON SUFFERING

I have written *Winks from Scripture* to serve two purposes.

First, the winks illustrate that there is always more than meets the eye. What God is doing is usually not obvious to us at first, if ever. We shouldn't assume that God isn't at work because we can't pinpoint where He is or measure out all that He is doing.

Second, these winks help us to develop a theology of suffering in the New Testament narratives. I have chosen the winks for this purpose because suffering is a concept that evades our understanding. All the theologizing and philosophizing in the world cannot scratch the itch of our wondering about the problem of evil. We believers must appeal to mystery.

Yes, suffering is a mystery, but that doesn't mean that God, through Christ, hasn't done something or isn't doing something about it. There must be more in every account of suffering. For us to have hope, we must believe that God is doing something beyond what we can see. The winks provide evidence that God has been doing just that. He's at work, whether we see Him or not. And our hope is sustained.

Here I shall offer a wink from Scripture showing that God does more than meets the eye. It gives us hope in our suffering. In John 8:3–5, the scribes and Pharisees bring a woman who was caught in adultery to Jesus. They ask Jesus if they should stone her. John gives us an odd detail. If we haven't read the story before, it's unexpected. *"Jesus bent down and wrote with his finger on the ground"* (verse 6). The leaders are provoking Jesus, a woman's life is on the line, and Jesus just doodles on the ground? The religious leaders press Him further and, again, John records that Jesus just writes on the ground (verse 8).

Readers might wonder, *What does this mean? Is writing on the ground symbolic? Is dirt symbolic? Is it like God writing the Law on clay tablets with His finger? What language was He writing in? Would the religious leaders have understood what He was writing? Is the dirt a reference to mankind's creation in Genesis 2:7?*

I used to rush to explain John 8:6. I felt comfortable saying that Jesus was likely writing part of Jeremiah 17:13, which says, "O Lord, the hope of Israel…those who turn away from you shall be written in the earth." This would be an indictment on the religious leaders.

It's also been proposed that Jesus was writing, *"You shall not spread a false report. You shall not join hands with a wicked man to be a malicious witness"* (Exodus 23:1). Or perhaps Jesus was listing the religious leaders' sins. I even heard one minister say that Jesus was listing the names of the women with whom the religious leaders had fornicated.

The problem with these and other explanations is that there's no way to prove any of them. I have to throw my hands up and say, "I have no clue what Jesus was writing. Nobody does."

But that is just the point! We need to make room for a little twilight here. In allowing this one detail to be mysterious, ten thousand things become clear.

John didn't care to tell us what Jesus was writing. The missing detail places a mysterious aura around Jesus. It gives us the impression that Jesus is one step ahead of everyone. He's unpredictable. There's no putting *Him* into a box. Everyone is left wondering, *What is Jesus going to do next?* We discover a Jesus whom we can't predict and a God who can't be pinned down. Who knows what He is about to do?

The story winks. Although we don't know what God is up to, we do know He is working for our good. And Jesus works for this woman's good. He comes through for her in her suffering. Part of the beauty of this Scripture is that we don't have the details. We don't know how He did it.

This illustrates something about life and our encounters with the divine. How often has God come through for you, for us, and for His whole creation, with none of us knowing exactly how He did it? It's a mystery. But the mysterious God is working on our behalf. And in our suffering and pain, when we are far from knowing, we can trust that Jesus is writing on the ground. Whatever He's doing, we know it is to help us in time of need.

> IN OUR SUFFERING AND PAIN, WHEN WE ARE
> FAR FROM KNOWING, WE CAN TRUST THAT
> JESUS IS WRITING ON THE GROUND.

When we allow the biblical story to be a mystery, and when we are content with our own experiences being a mystery, the God we cannot predict will continue to surprise us in ways we don't expect as long as we don't stop looking and searching.

I need to give a disclaimer here. My *Winks from Scripture* are just that—winks. There's probably way more than the thirty I share. They cannot account for *all* that God is doing. They don't account for all that Scripture is saying, nor can they explain how we will use them to examine suffering. But again, they aren't supposed to. If anything, they serve as small confirmations that *God is here and at work*. Whether we notice Him or not, He is here, and He's doing something to reconcile the broken world to Himself. That is all that the story needs.

I hope this study will encourage you in your own suffering and somehow assure you that the story, your story, is fuller than you might imagine. Scripture says more. Your own experiences say more. God is winking at you. Perhaps the winks might give you hope in a hopeless situation. Could your own story offer you a wink, a nice little surprise that could stir hope, even delight? If the biblical narratives are our example, there is a good chance. Keep hope alive.

Finally, I must be careful not to oversimplify suffering or group all suffering together as the same. Suffering is a complex topic. I never realized just *how* complex until I focused my doctoral research on suffering and theodicy in the book of Revelation.

As we seek to understand God's subtle work among us, we cannot overlook how He comes alongside us in our suffering—as He did, for reasons known only to Him, with the pigeon that I encountered.

Suffering is the experience of any pain, no matter its source or whether is it emotional, physical, mental, relational, or spiritual.

The problem of suffering resists an intellectual solution. Observing the narrative elements of the story and putting together winks to point out the work of God in our suffering cannot do away with its sting, nor solve the conundrum of *why* we suffer. This is a mystery.

The *why* behind our suffering should be left alone. Pursuing scholarship on this subject is never enough. It is not a theological, philosophical, or scientific enterprise. Approaching it in this manner can yield helpful reflections to *offer hope*, but it never gets to the bottom of things. It will never answer *why*.

The biblical writers never sought to answer *why*. To them, the surprising thing was *not* that we suffer, but rather that we don't suffer *more* than we do. They understood the fall of man, our broken state, and the evil within us because of sin. What amazed them was the mercy of God toward us in our condition, not the fact that we suffer. (See Nehemiah 9:17; Psalm 103:8–18; Jonah 4:2.)

So why should we even pursue a study in suffering if it remains a problem that cannot be solved? It is fruitful if we approach it as the biblical authors approached it. In dealing with suffering, they put together what I call a *practical theodicy.*

Theodicy comes from the Greek words for *God* and *justice*, meaning "the justice of God." The term was first coined by Gottfried Wilhelm von Leibniz, an eighteenth-century German philosopher. The purpose of a theodicy is to vindicate God's goodness and justice in view of suffering and pain.

> THE BIBLICAL WRITERS NEVER SOUGHT TO ANSWER WHY WE SUFFER. INSTEAD, THEY TAUGHT GOD'S PEOPLE HOW TO FOLLOW HIM DESPITE SUFFERING.

A theodicy doesn't openly exist in Scripture. Paul, Moses, and Samuel never sat down and wrote a philosophical exposition on the matter. Instead, they taught God's people how to follow Him *despite* suffering. This is what I call a practical theodicy—instructions on how to live as God's people in a world where suffering is our lot and where we might suffer even more one day. It accepts the mystery without becoming hateful toward God or suspicious of His goodness. It focuses on how to please God and, as sufferers, to trust God and to trust in the day when He comes and brings His eschatological justice to right all wrongs.

The Bible places suffering between its two accounts of creation. In Genesis 1–2, we read that God has created a perfect world that has no suffering or evil. In Revelation 21–22, we find the re-creation of the world, a perfect place without suffering or evil. Things begin without suffering, and things end without suffering. But between these two creations, there *is* suffering.

TWO THINGS TO KNOW ABOUT SUFFERING

GOD DIDN'T CREATE SUFFERING

Suffering, as found between the creation and re-creation of the world, tells us two important things. *The first thing* is that God did not create suffering. He did not inflict pain on His creation. Suffering entered the world through sin.

Sin is evil because it's rebellion against the ways of God. In one sense, evil can be viewed as the transgressions we commit against one another and God that are harmful and injurious.

In another sense, there is something far more sinister behind these acts of rebellion and offense. The apostle Paul calls it *"the mystery of lawlessness"* (2 Thessalonians 2:7). There is an unseen fountain of darkness that champions the cause of rebellion and offense toward God. Even the apostle Peter was not immune to the influence of demonic powers. (See Matthew 16:23.) Much suffering comes as the direct result of these forces. Paul wrote:

> *We do not wrestle against flesh and blood, but against the rulers, against the authorities, against the cosmic powers over this present darkness, against the spiritual forces of evil in the heavenly places.* (Ephesians 6:12)

Consider everyday examples of suffering that happen in our neighborhoods because sinful humans are injurious toward one another—sins like theft, murder, rape, and adultery. Consider the grave suffering of wars, social evils, and things like child exploitation and sex trafficking that happen all over the world.

I've witnessed the effects of this unfathomable suffering on several occasions. In one instance, during Christmas 2019, I was in Kampala, Uganda, as part of a ministry that was feeding orphans and ministering in the local congregations. One afternoon, we went into the small villages outside of Kampala that Joseph Kony and the misnamed Lord's Resistance Army (LRA), a guerrilla group, had ravaged by abducting children to be soldiers and sex slaves. The children we met were starving and showed signs of extreme malnutrition.

Their untold suffering resulted from evil at work and the sin inside Kony and the LRA, on top of the political and social corruption that the landlocked countries in East Africa face regularly. These victims suffer because of the evil at work and the sin inside of someone else.

Yet suffering because of someone's sin doesn't explain tragedies such as car accidents, children's illnesses, tsunamis, life-ending cancers, or other cases in which no one has purposely transgressed against another.

For example, during the weekend of his wedding, my friend, his fiancée, and their families were waiting for his three sisters to show up for the rehearsal dinner. When the girls didn't arrive, they knew something was wrong. Soon afterward, they got word that the three had been killed in a head-on collision with a semitruck. Neither driver was drunk. No sin was involved. How do you even process that?

When I worked in pastoral care for a local church, I visited members and their families in the hospital. The most difficult visits always took place at the children's hospitals.

There was one particular child, about seven years old, who left a lasting impression on me. He was kind, articulate, and sweet.

He won my heart on the first visit. He was in the hospital because he suffered from lesions on his spine. I have a vivid memory of his walking from his bed to the bathroom in awful pain, needing his father's assistance. I felt helpless. All I could do was pray with him and his father and do my best to encourage them before I left. No matter how often I came to visit, I always left feeling something was deeply wrong. I would get in my car and agonize, crying out to God for answers.

How should we look at this? Evil and sin have left our world wretched and broken. Tragedy can happen—does happen—to everyone. Christian or non-Christian, tragedy is indiscriminate.

Children get sick, people die in car accidents, cancer kills, and earthquakes take lives because we live *between* Genesis 1:1 and Revelation 22:21. We live in a state of imperfection between two perfections. Though innocent suffering may not be the *direct* result of someone's sin and evil, the brokenness of our world *because* of sin and evil makes it a possibility. This means that, indirectly, tragic suffering results from evil and offense toward God. Whether it is *direct* suffering at the hands of a malevolent will or *indirect* tragic suffering that happens unrelated to any specific evil offense, sin and evil are the *ultimate* cause.

THOUGH INNOCENT SUFFERING MAY NOT BE THE DIRECT RESULT OF SOMEONE'S SIN AND EVIL, THE BROKENNESS OF OUR WORLD BECAUSE OF SIN AND EVIL MAKES IT A POSSIBILITY.

In our agony, Christ bids us to turn our hope away from this world and put it in Him, the One who declares, *"Behold, I am making all things new"* (Revelation 21:5) and *"Repent and believe in the gospel"* (Mark 1:15).

Don't put your trust in a world where children suffer, and accidents kill three sisters who want to help their brother prepare for his wedding. Don't bet on a world where manipulators stake out the innocent, and the powerful take advantage of the powerless. Bet on Christ.

GOD WORKS AGAINST SUFFERING

The second thing we should observe from the fact that suffering takes place between the creation of the universe (Genesis 1–2) and the re-creation of all things (Revelation 21–22) is that all of God's activity in between takes place *alongside* evil and suffering. He didn't just leave us to our misfortune and turn to another corner of the universe to start a better project.

God honed in on our suffering. He went to work against it. He enacted a plan to deliver humanity from its despair. As we trace salvation history from the Old Testament into the New Testament, we see this plan leading to His joining us in our suffering. He became the victim of the evil that causes our own suffering. Unlike us, as God, He did what we could not do and overcame the evil that wronged Him, thus defeating it. By experiencing suffering through evil, He overwhelmed both. His plan outdid the plan of evil.

The outworking of God's plan, which culminated in Christ, shows that God knows how to rework suffering. He can take what is meant to harm us and turn it into something that becomes useful for our good. This shows the power of His goodness and attests to His glory.

Joseph the Dreamer identifies this power and penchant of God. His brothers commit a great evil against him by selling him into slavery in Egypt. Yet, through providential events, Joseph becomes the prime minister of Egypt, spares his brothers' lives, and distributes food to them during a famine. He tells his brothers, *"As for you, you meant evil against me, but God meant it for good, to bring it about that many people should be kept alive, as they are today"* (Genesis 50:20).

Joseph's statement is not only a statement about his own situation, but it also serves the bigger narrative about what God is doing about evil and suffering in this world. He is reworking it to conform to His glory, until all things become good and are new. While we live in this darkened state of imperfection between the two states of perfection, we can trust that God is at work against suffering and its source, evil and sin. As Paul said, *"And we know that for those who love God all things work together for good, for those who are called according to his purpose"* (Romans 8:28).

CHRISTIAN SUFFERING

There is a form of suffering that is unique to Christians: suffering for the name of Christ through persecution. The New Testament contains plentiful references to this. The apostles tell us that persecution and suffering for Christ are par for the course when we follow Him. (See Acts 5:41; Philippians 1:29; 2 Timothy 1:8; 1 Peter 4:12–16.) Jesus even discouraged His disciples from following Him if they did not foresee the suffering for His sake that they would experience. (See Luke 9:23–27.)

Christian suffering, caused by persecution, results from direct evil. The people of God suffer because their devotion to God contrasts with the evil that is in the world. There is friction.

This friction intensified when Jesus inaugurated His kingdom, calling for the total obedience and complete fidelity of His followers. Offering this fidelity is bothersome to the world because faithfulness to Christ is an inherent protest against how the world thinks and acts. Jesus identified this issue when He said, *"Do not think that I have come to bring peace to the earth. I have not come to bring peace, but a sword"* (Matthew 10:34). Jesus is not calling for holy war; He is saying that being His disciple will create friction and stir things up.

This is inevitable if the kingdom coexists alongside a fallen and broken world. The disciples soon discovered this. It wasn't long after the day of Pentecost that they received their first beating. (See Acts 5:40–41.) Soon afterward, the first Christian martyr, Stephen, was stoned to death. (See Acts 7:54–60.)

The persecution of Christians has not stopped since then, nor will it. Due to the advancement of human rights and democratic governments, many Christians today experience minimal persecution compared to what the apostles faced. But there are still millions of Christians in persecuted countries who lose their lives because of the gospel. Their suffering is the result of evil.

Like Christ, those who are persecuted to death overcome evil *in* their own death. Peter wrote, *"And after you have suffered a little while, the God of all grace, who has called you to his eternal glory in Christ, will himself restore, confirm, strengthen, and establish you"* (1 Peter 5:10).

In the kingdom of God, sufferers overcome through their suffering. What the persecutors mean for evil, God turns into good— He triumphs through suffering, as do all who lay down their lives with Him.

Christ has power to right all wrongs and defeat evil *because* He was slain. (See Revelation 5:9–12.) By becoming the victim of evil, He overcame evil. Those who suffer for Christ bear witness to this. This is the subversive nature of Christ's kingdom. In suffering evil at the hands of evil, evil loses.

SUFFERING WITH GOD'S DISCIPLINE

The last form of suffering we will examine is God's discipline toward His people. The Scriptures tell us:

"For the Lord disciplines the one he loves, and chastises every son whom he receives." It is for discipline that you have to

endure. God is treating you as sons. For what son is there whom his father does not discipline? If you are left without discipline, in which all have participated, then you are illegitimate children and not sons. Besides this, we have had earthly fathers who disciplined us and we respected them. Shall we not much more be subject to the Father of spirits and live? For they disciplined us for a short time as it seemed best to them, but he disciplines us for our good, that we may share his holiness. For the moment all discipline seems painful rather than pleasant, but later it yields the peaceful fruit of righteousness to those who have been trained by it.   (Hebrews 12:6–11)

In a sense, God's discipline is a form of suffering because it's uncomfortable, it can be painful, and it may place us in a season of discomfort. But this differs greatly from suffering caused by evil. Evil is cold-hearted, spiteful, and malicious. It seeks to harm people, take advantage of them, and disrespect the image of God in which they were created.

Discipline is not evil, for it comes from love and seeks a person's good. There is an obvious difference between the pain of a villager attacked by guerrilla fighters and the pain a disobedient child experiences when his father takes away his cell phone.

Note *where and when* God's discipline occurs. There is no indication that humankind needed discipline before the fall. Adam and Eve were given rules to follow, but God did not discipline them until after they broke those rules through their sin. (See Genesis 3:14–19.) Furthermore, there is no indication that discipline will be used by God to correct the redeemed in the new heaven and the new earth. Instead, we learn that God *"will wipe away every tear from their eyes, and death shall be no more, neither shall there be mourning, nor crying, nor pain anymore, for the former things have passed away"* (Revelation 21:4).

God's discipline takes place in our imperfect world, between both creations. The reality of sin and evil has necessitated God's correction. But because both cause some level of pain, we shouldn't make the mistake of confusing God's necessary correction with the evil that has made it necessary.

> ## WE SHOULDN'T MAKE THE MISTAKE OF CONFUSING GOD'S NECESSARY CORRECTION WITH THE EVIL THAT HAS MADE IT NECESSARY.

God doesn't make it His mission to harm us. Instead, He will perfect us through evil already conveyed toward us or by us. Thus, He takes what was meant for evil and reworks it for His good.

Let's look at a couple examples. If one of God's children has been cheating on taxes and is caught by the IRS, God may permit that person to be penalized no matter how hard they pray. The penalty, be it a large fine or jail time, might be the discomfort God allows to perfect the offender. Though the offender suffers because they are locked up, God did not create the evil. It is a consequence of the person's own evil, which God *allows* to perfect the person *from* evil.

We find another example of God's discipline in Scripture. The apostle Paul says, *"So to keep me from becoming conceited because of the surpassing greatness of the revelations, a thorn was given me in the flesh, a messenger of Satan to harass me"* (2 Corinthians 12:7).

It seems like a riddle. At first glance, it's easy to think that God gave Paul the thorn in the flesh that the apostle called *"a messenger of Satan."* Is this what was really going on? Was God working through Satan to discipline Paul and keep him from being boastful? It seems oversimplified to say so, plus it puts God in league with evil. It is better to suggest that God reworked Paul's suffering, which came as a thorn in the flesh, to perfect him, thus getting glory by turning what Satan meant for evil to serve God's purpose of good. In this sense, Paul thought of it as a gift from the Lord.

It is possible to conclude this by examining the words *"was given"* in the text. This comes from the Greek word *edothē*, which is the verb for "give" found in the passive voice. The passive voice hides the doer of the action—in this case, God. When the passive voice is used referring to God's actions, it is known as a "divine passive." The purpose is to indicate that God is indirectly involved in an action. He's behind the scenes.

There may be situations in our own lives that seem injurious. Yet, instead of making these things go away, God allows them in order to discipline us and perfect us. In this regard, they *are* a gift from the Lord, yet at the same time, God is not doing evil or working through evil. He is simply behind the scenes *reworking* evil for our own good.

REJECTING DUALISM

Before ending our brief study on suffering, it is important to discuss the concept of dualism, the belief that there are two equally opposed forces at work in the universe: good and evil. This is seen in the Chinese concept of yin and yang, which posits that two opposing forces are intertwined to give balance to one another. In the Western world, we are familiar with dualism through movies like *Star Wars*, in which Siths, devoted to the dark side of the Force, battle Jedis, who are devoted to the light.

Unfortunately, these concepts have influenced our thinking as Bible readers. There is a tendency to see the people of God as Jedi knights and Satan's kingdom as Siths. While Scripture does teach that "light" and "darkness" are at work (see John 1:5), it is not dualistic in the classic sense—because nowhere in the Bible are these opposing forces seen as equals. God is omnipotent. Period. At no point in the biblical text does evil have any chance of prevailing over God's sovereignty. God always defeats it handily.

With this said, we can understand that the evil directly and indirectly causing our suffering has occurred within the realm of God's sovereignty. Everything that has taken place between two creations, in this imperfect state, has been permitted by God. Evil didn't creep in without God knowing it. It would be dualistic to think so, for it would suggest that God suffered some defeat.

While it seems comforting to know that God is sovereign over evil, this is where the problem lies. Why does God permit evil if He is all-powerful over it? This point brings us full circle, back to the problem of suffering—a problem, as I noted previously, that we can never solve intellectually.

D. A. Carson makes a valuable point that is worth considering. He writes, "In God's universe, even Satan cannot step outside the boundaries of God's sovereignty. While that is what raises the problem, it is also what promises hope."[2]

Though what stumps us is the omnipotence of God allowing evil, the omnipotence of God is also what gives us hope. It assures us that evil has lost—and *is* losing. Evil will never ultimately triumph. The plan that God has enacted to join in our suffering and make us victors has won the day. We have sure hope of a future without pain and evil. We live in an imperfect world, between two perfect creations, while God works behind the scenes to make everything right. In this there is mystery, and there is hope. And, at times, God winks and reminds us it is so.

THE LENS OF SUFFERING

The gospel is the story of God, through Christ Jesus, outdoing the plan of evil through His omnipotence while experiencing the suffering of mankind and triumphing. It is chock-full of hope

---

2. D. A. Carson, *How Long, O Lord? Reflections on Suffering and Evil* (Grand Rapids, MI: Baker Academic, 2006), 140. Carson's work is one of many that have influenced some of my thinking. For more on suffering, *How Long, O Lord?* would be a good place to begin.

but riddled with mystery. It is an ironic paradox. The whole story is incongruous and contrary to everything the first century world knew at the time. This is why the Jews stumbled at the story of Jesus and the Greeks mocked it. (See 1 Corinthians 1:23.) The gospel is a mysterious victory over suffering and evil.

THE GOSPEL IS THE STORY OF GOD, THROUGH CHRIST JESUS, OUTDOING THE PLAN OF EVIL THROUGH HIS OMNIPOTENCE WHILE EXPERIENCING THE SUFFERING OF MANKIND AND TRIUMPHING.

In the devotional studies that follow, I approach the gospel by:

+ *Appreciating the gospel as a story.* In each study, I examine different stories within the gospel passages and some of the elements that I mention in my preface. These yield ironies, absurdities, and intimations—what I call *winks.*

+ *Using the winks in the story to appreciate ambiguity and mystery.* The winks that surprise us are subtle and, to a degree, hidden. These serve as a good place to explore a theology of suffering because God's work against suffering in our own lives is also, to a degree, hidden. Noting God's reticence and inscrutability in the gospel stories can be illustrative of our own lives, where we don't often recognize when God is at work, *especially* when we are suffering. If answers are available, they aren't often obvious. The winks confirm this. They can teach us, as followers of Christ, to be at peace with God working behind the scenes, whether we eventually get answers or not. Mystery is okay. It should excite us, not discourage us, and should teach us that there is more meaning in our own experiences than we realize. Therefore, we can trust God.

+ *Appreciating the work of God amid the mystery of suffering and evil.* Many of the texts within New Testament narratives deal with suffering either explicitly or implicitly. In some way, they point to God at work in our suffering, working against the evil that has directly or indirectly caused it, and reworking the suffering to perfect us.

+ Unlike certain sects that try to erase suffering from Scripture as though it is not supposed to be part of a Christian's life or those who glorify suffering as though it *is* the desired end of spiritual life, this study accepts suffering as a mysterious part of life that affects believers and nonbelievers alike. Winks offer only as many answers as the story surprises us with and allows, which unfortunately is not enough to satisfy us intellectually.

+ There is still a lot of room for mystery. Yet, this study gladly accepts the mystery. It welcomes the uncertainty—because when we are wavering, we can be certain that God is at work doing far more than we expect. He's winking at us in Scripture, and this offers us hope and gives us confidence that there is a time coming when everything will be made right. Everything is in the process of *being* made right. We are living between two perfections, and the final perfection is coming. (See 1 Corinthians 13:10.)

+ *Offering insights in devotional form.* Few people tend to read books on mystery and suffering because they can be exhausting and dense. Take it from someone who has a stack of theology books on these subjects that reaches from floor to ceiling. The best chance I have at getting someone to consider these things is in an encouraging, easy-to-read devotional—like this one.

We will rarely know what God is doing. We might scratch our heads and wonder what He's up to—if He's up to anything. But if we keep asking questions about the mysterious, every now and again, we will catch a wink. We'll be reminded that God is good.

Keep your eyes peeled. The text is winking at you. Your experiences are winking at you. What beautiful things God is doing in the mystery! Some, we just might discover, are both here and now.

Maranatha.

μαρανα θα

Chris Palmer

Wink #1

GOD WINKS IN THE RE-CREATION

In 2018, I stood in one of Cambodia's "killing fields" in Phnom Penh and wrestled with my Christian faith. If you are not familiar with the term "killing field," it refers to one of a number of sites in Cambodia where the Khmer Rouge regime, under the leadership of Pol Pot, executed over two million of its own people between 1975 and 1979.

My tour was self-guided, with an audio headset that explained the stations built along the way. The horror I was confronted with culminated when the headset instructed me to stop in front of a large tree that stood along the path. The soothing voice of the narrator was no comfort in explaining how this very tree was used in the execution of tens of thousands of innocent Cambodians, including babies.

Since I was the only one on this part of the tour, nobody saw the color drain from my face. My knees got weak. I wept.

I mustered enough resolution to finish the tour, but not before I was faced with a two-hundred-foot tower of human skulls. Over eight thousand heads in this memorial were retrieved from the field. These were once living people like you and like me. They had dreams, fears, and families. They had questions about suffering. Many, I imagine, were wondering about God. *Where is He? Why is this happening? What kind of world have I been born into?* It still haunts me.

This was a seminal moment in my life, when I decided to begin my doctorate work on the topic of suffering. It would take at least five years to process what I had felt in that two-hour circuit. I didn't expect an answer. How could there be an answer this side of heaven? At least an academic journey might help me to work through my thinking.

I offer a sentiment from Scripture that this academic journey has yielded. Though it can offer no rationalization for the indescribable suffering of the Cambodian people, it does give us a reason to hope in God. He *will* vindicate the suffering of the innocent. The sentiment aims to show us that God hasn't abandoned us to evil. He is at work, in the evil and against the evil. He's alive. He's present in the darkness. The Christian faith posits that God's redemption has begun and will ultimately be realized in the age to come. We trust that His work today offers us joy that culminates tomorrow.

The Gospel of John speaks to this. There are winks within it confirming that God is re-creating the world through the work of Christ. As we trek through the narrative, we will see that John shows us that Jesus has joined us in our suffering. Through this work, Jesus redeems the world. He transforms the killing field into a garden of life.

Here is how John paints this picture. The first thing to notice is John's introduction of Christ:

> **In the beginning** was the Word, and the Word was with God, and the Word was God. He was in the beginning with God. All things were made through him, and without him was not any thing made that was made. **In him was life**, and the life

*was the light of men. **The light shines in the darkness**, and the darkness has not overcome it.*   (John 1:1–5)

The language in this introduction echoes the book of Genesis:

John	Genesis
In the beginning (1:1)	*In the beginning* (1:1)
The light shines in the darkness (1:5)	*Let there be light* (1:3)
In him was life (1:4)	*Let the earth bring forth living creatures* (1:24)

By echoing Genesis, John connects Jesus to it. He does this to proclaim that Jesus is the Creator. The One who walks with us is the One who created the world. He came with the purpose to create—only this time, He has come to *re-create* what evil and sin have destroyed.

> ## BY ECHOING GENESIS, JOHN CONNECTS JESUS TO IT AND PROCLAIMS THAT JESUS IS THE CREATOR.

The portrayal of Jesus as the re-creator finds its way through John. It intensifies during His work on the cross. There are six instances during Christ's passion where John winks and hints that Christ is re-creating. If we look at these winks, one by one, it *may seem* plausible that John is trying to tell us something. When we look at them together, it becomes hard to dismiss the idea that John is communicating something profound.

The first wink occurs after Jesus is flogged. The King of Kings is given a crown of thorns, He's robed in purple, and He is presented to the chief priests and officers. Pilate says to them, *"Behold the man!"* (John 19:5). While this may seem insignificant, could it suggest that Jesus is the "new man," the "second Adam," the beginning point of a new humanity? Genesis 1:27 tells us, *"So God created man in his own image."* Just as the first Adam was the focus of the first creation, so Jesus is the focus of the new creation.

The second wink occurs after Jesus drinks the sour wine. He says, *"It is finished"* (John 19:30), bows His head, and dies. *"It is finished"* comes from the Greek word *teleō*, which is used in the Septuagint to describe the finished work of creation:

> *Thus, the heavens and the earth were **finished** [synteleo], and all the host of them. And on the seventh day God **finished** [synteleo] his work that he had done, and he rested on the seventh day from all his work that he had done. So God blessed the seventh day and made it holy, because on it God rested from all his work that he had done in creation.*
>
> (Genesis 2:1–3)

Was John hinting that the work of this re-creation had been finished at the cross? In the next verse, he writes:

> *Since it was the day of Preparation, and so that the bodies would not remain on the cross on the Sabbath (for that Sabbath was a high day), the Jews asked Pilate that their legs might be broken and that they might be taken away.*
>
> (John 19:31)

The day of Preparation was the day that Jews made ready for the coming Sabbath. This is a deeply ironic statement. The finished work of Christ ushered in the Sabbath. Does this have a double meaning? Might John be intimating that the finished work of Christ completed the Father's work and, having completed it, ushered in the Sabbath of God's rest? Because it is finished, Christ rests, just as God rested on the seventh day after making the world. This also hints at John's Christology and suggests to us that Christ is doing the work of God in Genesis. Therefore, He's God.

In the third wink, John gives us an odd detail about where Christ is buried:

*Now in the place where he was crucified there was a **garden**, and in the garden a new tomb in which no one had yet been laid. So because of the Jewish day of Preparation, since the tomb was close at hand, they laid Jesus there.*

(John 19:41–42)

We are told that the tomb is in a garden. John is the only gospel writer to give us this detail. Perhaps it seems insignificant...unless it is part of the theology he is developing. John has been painting a picture of Christ as the re-creator of the world. Now he uses this detail to draw us back to the Genesis account. This time, he points to Eden, the place where humankind existed before sin and suffering entered. Is John signaling that the death and resurrection of Christ has brought forth redemption? Can His redemptive work transform the killing fields of this world into new Eden?

The fourth wink is even more surprising. After rising from the dead, Jesus finds Mary Magdalene crying outside of the tomb. He approaches Mary and asks why she is crying. The narrative tells us something interesting:

*Supposing him to be the **gardener**, she said to him, "Sir, if you have carried him away, tell me where you have laid him, and I will take him away."* (John 20:15)

Mary thought that Jesus was the *gardener*. John is such a careful narrator, he wouldn't add this detail if there wasn't a purpose for it. It's quite amusing. Was Mary hallucinating? How could she mistake the One she knew and followed for a gardener?

N. T. Wright says, "Mary's intuitive guess, that he must be the gardener, was wrong at one level and right, deeply right, at another. This is the new creation. Jesus is the beginning of it...Here he is: the new Adam, the gardener, charged with bringing the chaos of God's creation into new order, into flower, into fruitfulness."[3]

---

3. N. T. Wright, *John for Everyone: Part 2 Chapters 11-21* (Louisville, KY: Westminster John Knox Press, 2004), 146.

The fifth wink comes right on the heels of this. The disciples are in a home with the doors locked, and Jesus suddenly shows up in their midst. John tells us *when* this occurs:

> *On the evening of that day, **the first day of the week**, the doors being locked where the disciples were for fear of the Jews, Jesus came and stood among them and said to them, "Peace be with you."* (John 20:19)

Jesus shows up on the first day of the week. Could this be suggesting that the resurrection of Christ has inaugurated a new *week* in human history, a week of re-creation when everything is being made new?

Finally and climactically, Scripture winks at us one more time. Christ is among His disciples, and He does something peculiar. We are told, "*He breathed on them and said to them, 'Receive the Holy Spirit'*" (John 20:22).

There have always been questions about what Jesus was doing when He breathed on the disciples. Those who read this think, *Were they receiving the Holy Spirit? If so, how is this different than what happens in Acts 2?*

The mystery is solved when we consider the Genesis narrative we've been tracking along with the Gospel of John. In light of the winks we've just seen, John calls us to Genesis one last time. Just as God breathed life into the Edenic couple during the first creation (see Genesis 2:7), so Christ breathes life into the disciples. In doing so, He launches the *new* creation.

Six winks:

1. "*Behold, the man*" (19:5)

2. "*It is finished*," and Christ's death prior to the Sabbath (19:30–31)

3. The tomb in the "garden" (19:41)

4. Mary mistakes Jesus for the "gardener" (20:15)

5. Jesus appears to His disciples on the first day of the week (20:19)

6. Jesus breathes on His disciples (20:22)

Each of these attests to John 1:1–5, where Christ is presented as Creator, but even more, they testify that He is the re-creator. These indicate to readers that Christ is up to something in redemption much larger than we realized.

While there is no possible way I could ever rationalize the horror I encountered while standing in the killing fields of Phnom Penh, perhaps it would have helped me to consider that God is in the center of our evil world, working against the terror that consumes us. The Scriptures lead us to know that we serve a God who hasn't left this suffering world to itself. He has begun to re-create. Redemption has sprung. Re-creation will continue until the killing fields become the garden He intended in Eden.

Until then, we can expect to see winks that God is at work in this mysterious, suffering life. These enable us to hope against hope until the final glorious day arrives when the work has culminated in our eternal joy:

> Then the angel showed me the river of the water of life, bright as crystal, flowing from the throne of God and of the Lamb through the middle of the street of the city; also, on either side of the river, the tree of life with its twelve kinds of fruit, yielding its fruit each month. The leaves of the tree were for the healing of the nations. No longer will there be anything accursed, but the throne of God and of the Lamb will be in it, and his servants will worship him. (Revelation 22:1–3)

Wink #2

GOD WINKS IN CHRIST'S SIGNS

As we consider the idea of suffering in Scripture, we need to pair it with the idea of Jesus Christ as re-creator. In our churches, we are taught that Jesus is Savior, Redeemer, and even our brother and friend. We need to be introduced to Him, extensively, as the one at work re-creating the world. A vigorous examination of this idea would help us when considering the suffering of humanity and the brokenness of our world.

One Friday night, I was driving along the freeway when traffic came to a halting stop. Traffic doesn't stop on a Friday night because of construction. There had to be an accident. After fifteen minutes of stop-and-go movement, I saw the ambulance lights. The fire trucks were arriving. The wreckage was fresh. A car had slid under a semitruck. The car's roof was peeled back, and the vehicle was mangled. I would have been surprised if there were any survivors.

Naturally, I thought about who was in the car, what their family must have done when they received the phone call, and how the truck driver must have felt. There was a lot to consider. It weighed heavily on me for days because I was in the process of writing this book. There were times when I caught myself wondering what I would say if I were the one officiating at the funeral.

A day before this accident, another tragedy had made national and international news. Part of a concrete building in Surfside, Florida, collapsed. The building contained 136 apartments, and 55 of them crumbled. The collapse took place at 1:30 a.m. when many tenants were asleep. Imagine being sound asleep in your bed when suddenly the ceiling above you caves in.

One of my close friends knew a young woman who lived in one of those apartments and was among the victims. He sent me her Instagram. Her most recent post had come just days before she perished. She was full of life. The eerie feeling crept up on me when I was glancing at her last post, taken at the beach. She was unaware that she would soon face a terrifying death. It's too much to think about. How would the rabbis and ministers and priests who eulogize the bereaved prepare their words? What can they say?

Nothing. That is the hardest part. God is silent.

And while God is silent, we are left to live in a world where a roof can cave in on any of us at any moment. Our car can slide under a truck on any day of the week. We are here today, gone tomorrow.

We think, *Something is truly wrong with life.* This is the closest thing to an answer that any of us will get. Life is messed up.

In time, this reality will hit us in the face over and over again. Give it a few more days, weeks, months, and another event will remind you just how menacing life is. And what will we make of God? We only have three options:

1. God is all powerful but not good.

2. God is good but not all powerful.

3. God is good *and* all powerful, but He cannot be understood, particularly in times of suffering.

Which will it be? Scripture teaches number three. In times of suffering, we choose to believe God *is* all-powerful *yet* still good. And while He cannot be understood in moments of car accidents and ceiling collapses, we can believe He is re-creating. And He must be working in the re-creating. Either He is fixing the human experience, or He is indifferent. And if He is indifferent, He is cruel.

The Gospel of John winks. No, He's not cruel—He's good. And in His all-powerfulness, He's restoring the world.

We see this wink through the course of John's gospel, in the signs that Jesus performs. The first sign that Jesus performed is turning the water into wine at the wedding feast at Cana. (See John 2:1–12.) John literally tells his readers this is the "first" of Christ's signs: *"This, the first of his signs, Jesus did at Cana in Galilee, and manifested his glory. And his disciples believed in him"* (verse 11).

The second sign Jesus performs is healing an official's son who *"was at the point of death"* (John 4:47). John literally tells his readers this was the "second" of his signs: *"This was now the second sign that Jesus did when he had come from Judea to Galilee"* (verse 54).

John has made it a point to count off the first two signs of Jesus. This is an indicator to his readers that they should continue counting them as the narrative moves forward. As we do, we will notice something peculiar about the number of signs that John shares.

"*The first of his signs*"	2:1–11	Turns water into wine
"*The second sign*"	4:46–54	Heals official's son
Third sign	5:1–9	Heals a disabled man
Fourth sign	6:1–15	Feeds five thousand
Fifth sign	6:16–21	Walks on water
Sixth sign	9:1–7	Heals a man born blind
Seventh sign	11:1–44	Raises Lazarus from the dead

It is striking that John's gospel recounts seven signs that Jesus performs until the time of His resurrection. Seven is the number of creation. Once again, John echoes the Genesis account. These seven signs point to God, the Creator who made the world. (See Genesis 1:1–2:3.) They testify to John 1:1–5 and present Jesus as this Creator, the One who made all things. They show He has dominion over the elements and power over sickness. From Him comes abundant provision. He even has power over death. In this messed-up world where things go wrong, He is Lord. And to this messed-up world, the good Lord re-creates all things.

JOHN'S GOSPEL RECOUNTS SEVEN SIGNS THAT JESUS PERFORMS UNTIL THE TIME OF HIS RESURRECTION, ONCE AGAIN ECHOING THE GENESIS ACCOUNT.

What is more interesting is that Jesus performs another sign besides these: His own resurrection from the dead. In John 2:18, the Jews question His credentials after He drove the money-changers and merchants out of the temple. They ask Him for a sign. Jesus says, *"Destroy this temple, and in three days I will raise it up"* (verse 19).

While His resurrection could be seen as the eighth sign that Jesus performs in John's gospel, it serves the narrative better to suggest that it is the *first* sign *after* the seven signs of re-creation. In His ministry, He begins re-creation. In His resurrection, He inaugurates it. The solution for the world's chaos culminates in the resurrection of Christ. It marks the beginning of life set free from suffering, a life that death can never threaten.

Amidst falling buildings, tragic car wrecks, and the deepest sufferings we experience, Christ invites us to be part of this new creation He has launched. This is God's original intent for humans. In it, we receive hope for life that extends beyond suffering and the consequences of evil.

This requires faith and the help of the Holy Spirit to believe, especially when suffering surprises us and attempts to suffocate our hopefulness. The next time suffering and tragedy confront you, ask the Holy Spirit for grace. Acknowledge there is something deeply wrong with this world, but remind yourself that the Scripture winks in Jesus's signs. The resurrection has opened the new creation to us.

The re-creator invites us into it.

Wink #3

GOD WINKS IN THE PRACTICAL

By now it's clear that suffering is a mysterious riddle that never goes away. Our most brilliant minds have tried to explain it. But explaining theodicy is like rubbing out a deep stain. Soap. Scrub. Rinse. Soap. Scrub. Rinse. The stain remains bold as ever. Glaring at you, unfazed by the best solution you offer, mocking you. *Is that the best you got?* Volumes have been written about why our loving and all-powerful God allows suffering. Scores of sermons have been preached. Brilliant lectures have been given. The riddle still taunts us.

It's said in philosophy, "There is no satisfying theodicy." As one who's written a thesis on it, I would agree.

So, what do we do when our intellect lets us down?

First, a bit of history: Christians have acknowledged the problem of evil and suffering since the days of the early church. More modern attempts to understand evil through reason and philosophy owe their origins to the Enlightenment of the seventeenth and eighteenth centuries. During this period, humanity relied on science and rationale. The world became skeptics. Christians were left in a conundrum. Evil in the world demanded a rational explanation to defend the goodness of God. Rich, timeless reflections about evil and suffering were born, but still, no satisfying answer to explain *why*.

Four hundred years after the Enlightenment, we are still standing upon the shore, looking into the darkness of the night, and asking questions that evade our logic. We need to do this. But the winks we catch come up short of answering the riddle *why*. It's not what we are accustomed to in the age of information. We want answers because science and reason make us believe that uncertainty is an enemy. And yet the mystery of suffering and evil remains outside of the human ability to *know*.

I was frustrated with this notion when I began my thesis. Call it ambition, but I thought I'd make a dent in this area of study. Could I solve the riddle? It didn't take long to give in. No one had done it—not G. K. Chesterton, not Fyodor Dostoevsky, not Søren Kierkegaard, not Jürgen Moltmann. If these great minds could not tell us *why*, how could I end up any differently?

However, I did make one observation: There is nothing in Scripture that explains evil and suffering. When Job stares into the mystery and asks God about it, all he gets are more questions. (See Job 38–41.) Revelation, the most theodicean book in the whole New Testament, deals with the problem of evil in just about every verse…yet without rational explanation.

So what does this mean?

 SCRIPTURE ACCEPTS THE MYSTERY OF EVIL AND SUFFERING WHILE RELINQUISHING ANY OPPORTUNITY TO EXPLAIN. INSTEAD, IT ENCOURAGES BELIEVERS TO ENDURE.

Scripture accepts the mystery of evil and suffering. It relinquishes any opportunity to explain. Instead, it encourages believers to endure, given what God is doing to redeem humankind. While there are benefits to approaching the problem of evil with science and reason, our deepest meditations should be on what Scripture *does* reveal—there is evil in the world, God has done something about it through Christ, God's plan remains in action, and we must hope in Him until He comes again with divine justice. We can hope and act on this, even if we never have a deeper explanation.

In the Gospel of Mark, the problem of evil and suffering is presented in a rather interesting way. Mark neither explains it nor rationalizes it. Instead, he subtly drops it in the narrative as a reality that contends against the ministry of Jesus. It serves as a wink to us that evil does exist alongside of God, but never equal to God. Jesus is at work in it, faithfully executing the Father's plans. And we don't have to explain it. Our inability to rationalize the problem of evil doesn't invalidate what God is doing about it, as the ministry of Jesus shows.

We begin in Mark 1. Here, the ministry of Jesus gets started with an exorcism in the synagogue. He drives out an evil spirit that knows who Jesus is, for he says, *"What have you to do with us, Jesus of Nazareth? Have you come to destroy us? I know who you are—the Holy One of God"* (Mark 1:24). After Jesus frees the man (see verses 25–26), He then proceeds to heal *"many who were sick with various diseases, and cast out many demons"* (verse 34).

The very next day, Jesus *"went throughout all Galilee, preaching in their synagogues and casting out demons"* (Mark 1:39). In the meanwhile, Jesus also heals Simon Peter's feverish mother-in-law and a leper. (See verses 30–31 and 40–45, respectively.)

In one chapter, Mark gives us multiple instances of a supernatural evil behind the woes and sufferings of humankind. This evil was in conflict with Jesus.

Next, in Mark 2–3, we find what appears to be a different sort of conflict. Jesus is no longer contested by demons. Instead, the scribes and Pharisees challenge Him three times. (See 2:6–7, 16, 24.) Eventually, they decide they must destroy Him. (See Mark 3:6.) Evil is at work.

After these scenes of the religious leaders opposing Jesus, we find demons contesting Him once more, falling down before Him and crying out, *"You are the Son of God"* (3:11).

The way the conflict is set up in Mark forms a literary device known as an *intercalation*. This involves interrupting a story by inserting a seemingly unrelated story into the middle of it. I like to call it "a literary sandwich." The story inserted into the middle enhances the theological interest of the story surrounding and often illustrating it.

Mark is notorious for using intercalations. This one in his first three chapters looks something like this:

- Part I: Demonic conflict (Mark 1:21–39)

    » *Intercalation:* Conflict with the religious leaders (2:6–3:1)

- Part II: Demonic conflict (3:11)

 MARK WINKS AT US WITH AN INTERCALATION, PLACING JESUS'S CONFLICT WITH THE RELIGIOUS LEADERS BETWEEN HIS CONFLICTS WITH THE DEMONIC.

Mark winks at us by placing Jesus's conflict with the religious leaders between His conflicts with the demonic. This illustrates that all are in league together—religious leaders with demons, demons with religious leaders. Mark wants us to see it all as the same thing: evil. This working of evil surrounded Jesus, whether it was a Pharisee who accused Him, a scribe who condemned Him, or a demon who taunted Him. And yet, we find Jesus in the center of it. He's working out the plan of God without offering any explanation for the evil that mocked Him.

He just fixed His eyes on the cross. He followed through with His mission. And He lived out His service toward His Father. There's no rationalizing. No measuring with scientific data. No heavy philosophy. His focus is the cross. He is about His Father's business.

At day's end, we can never explain why evil surrounds us. Fortunately, this isn't the goal. We don't observe Jesus giving His Sermon on the Mount to explain to the crowds why the Pharisees are evil or where demons come from. His exhortations in the Beatitudes contain the truth of how to live despite evil. He is concerned with a practical response to the problem of evil, not a philosophical response to it.

I'm not suggesting that evil shouldn't perplex or trouble us. It certainly should. We stand and face the mystery with our questions, in the hopes of receiving a wink. Whatever your rationale gets, that's great. A rich reflection? Wonderful. A profound meditation? Splendid. At the end of the day, whatever we know or don't know, God expects us to follow Christ, who works while suffering. Put simply, we should put our hope and trust in what we *do* know: God is at work.

The Gospel of Mark winks at us and tells us that evil will surround us in various forms. Perhaps it will be an overt demonic attack or a person who causes untold trouble. When you find yourself in the midst of evil, you can find hope in knowing that Jesus has done something about it.

How will you respond to the evil in your world when you find yourself in the thick of it? Instead of putting total trust in the Enlightenment route, pondering the deep mysteries of it, you can follow the biblical route.

The Scripture winks. Live as though Christ has done something about it—because He has. It doesn't *have* to be any more profound than that.

Wink #4

GOD WINKS IN THE DARKNESS

Where is God in all of this?

Where you least expect Him to be.

I tell my students that God isn't a firefly that they can catch in a jar. We can't capture His ways. There's no catching the One who created existence. No chance of controlling the One who holds the world in His hands. The Sovereign Lord evades our figuring Him out. When we spot Him, it's only because He chose to make Himself known for that moment in time. Then, He hides. He leaves us wondering where He'll show up next.

The journey of faith is the catching of flickers. Like the dancing of fireflies on a dark summer night, He shows up, then He's gone. These subtle, luminous winks of radiance into our lives leave us with a sense of awe, anticipating the next wink that will signal He's out there somewhere, working in the darkness. We'd get bored with Him if we could put Him in a jar. We could even end up resenting Him a bit.

Faith is the eager anticipation of seeing God wink once more. He will. But never when or where we might expect. This is a difficult concept to grasp in our day and age. We're so accustomed to having answers at the tip of our fingers. It can be a bit unsettling to realize that we do not know where God is, what He is doing, or how He might show up next.

 IT CAN BE A BIT UNSETTLING TO REALIZE THAT WE DO NOT KNOW WHERE GOD IS, WHAT HE IS DOING, OR HOW HE MIGHT SHOW UP NEXT.

I get a bit frustrated when I hear so much certainty in some preachers' sermons today. Sure, there are things we can say with assurance—there are sixty-six books in the Bible, Jesus died for our sins, and salvation comes by grace through faith. But there are things we can't know.

Can our relationship survive this betrayal? Will my mother beat her fight with cancer? Why do kids in developing countries—and many developed ones—starve to death? No preacher on any pulpit can give you a thorough answer without its ending in a cringe.

It's better to accept the mystery. Better to shed our oversimplified matter-of-factness for *real faith*, which is trusting that God is somehow at work in the darkness. It's standing on the shore and not being intimidated by the blackness of the night. It's saying, "I can't see You, but I know You're there."

The darkness stares back. No give. No empathy. No signal of compassion. We keep coming back to face the night sky, to gaze into mystery.

Then, one night, after countless of nights of nothingness, a burst of light splits the dense veil. The cloudless, moonless night sky spreads out a blanket of millions of twinkling stars above you. It winks—and you feel gladness in your heart. There's something at work in the mystery. There's something alive in the chaos. Whatever's going on, there's reason to hope.

We can never predict when the darkness will wink. This keeps us looking. It makes us wonder. A wink invites us to trust the One at work in the darkness, though we hardly see at all. Choosing to do so is faith.

The gospel story as told by Mark winks at us from many of the events in Jesus's ministry. These often go overlooked by readers, especially if they are not following the story closely. In this study, we notice that the story winks to us in Christ's darkest hour, at the time of His crucifixion. Here it *seems* that the Father may have abandoned Him:

> And at the ninth hour Jesus cried with a loud voice, "Eloi, Eloi, lema sabachthani?" which means, "My God, my God, why have you forsaken me?" (Mark 15:34)

To catch the wink, we need to examine this event in consideration of the whole story. There are two other main events leading up to this that are important to observe: Christ's baptism and His transfiguration.

The first major event of Christ's ministry is His baptism:

> In those days Jesus came from Nazareth of Galilee and was baptized by John in the Jordan. And when he came up out of the water, immediately he saw **the heavens being torn open** and the Spirit descending on him like a dove. And **a voice came** from heaven, "**You are my beloved Son**; with you I am well pleased." (Mark 1:9–11)

Here, it's easy to see that the Father is present: the heavens are torn open; an audible voice thunders from heaven; and the voice tells Christ He is the beloved Son. It's pretty obvious the Father is present at Christ's baptism, is it not?

Sometime later, Jesus takes Peter, James, and John up a high mountain, and He is *"transfigured before them, and his clothes became radiant, intensely white, as no one on earth could bleach them"* (Mark 9:2–3).

> *And a cloud overshadowed them, and a voice came out of the cloud, "This is my beloved Son; listen to him."*   (Mark 9:7)

Here we see similar indicators that the Father is present like He was at Jesus's baptism: a cloud moves in; an audible voice speaks from the cloud; and Jesus is called *"my beloved Son."* Again, these are pretty obvious signs that the Father is present.

By now in Mark's narrative, a pattern develops that acclimates the reader to what we should expect when the Father is present—torn heavens, clouds, a booming voice, and affirmation that Jesus is God's Son. By now, we know what to look for when God is at work. Or do we?

When we get to the crucifixion of Christ, we are presented with a dilemma:

> *And when the sixth hour had come, there was **darkness** over the whole land until the ninth hour. And at the ninth hour Jesus cried with a loud voice, "Eloi, Eloi, lema sabachthani" which means, "My God, my God, why have you forsaken me?"*   (Mark 15:33–34)

Jesus is at the darkest moment of His ministry. The cross is the climactic event of the whole story. Are the heavens going to tear? Will a voice boom from above? Will God affirm that Jesus is His beloved Son while He hangs on the cross for the sins of the world?

No. The heavens don't tear. A voice doesn't boom. There's no affirmation that Jesus is the beloved Son.

Instead, there is darkness, and the skies turn ominous. Jesus is all alone. And He prays a heartbreaking prayer from Psalm 22:1, lamenting the hour of His death. "God! Where are You? Why have You forsaken Me?"

Sound familiar? Does that sound like someone standing on the seashore, glaring into the darkness of the night while the waves pound the sand, wondering, *Where is God?* Nowhere to be found, it seems. As readers, we have been given clues that tell us what to expect when God is present. But none of these indicators are here.

> JUST WHEN WE THINK THE FATHER HAS ABANDONED THE SON, MARK'S GOSPEL GIVES US A WINK TO LET US KNOW HE IS STILL THERE.

Our initial reaction is sadness and disappointment. We think, *The Father has abandoned the Son.* The dark skies and lamentation are proof. This is the exact *opposite* of what we can foresee when God is present.

And with that thought, Mark has succeeded in his narration. Like a seasoned magician, his indirection becomes the most powerful element of his storytelling. While we, the readers, are grieving the dark skies and feeling horror-struck by the lamenting Christ, Mark gives us a wink, a subtle flicker of light that shows God is there in the darkness. He's alive in the chaos. Notice:

> *And Jesus uttered a loud cry and breathed his last. And **the curtain of the temple was torn in two**, from top to bottom.*
> (Mark 15:37–38)

In the distance, the temple curtain is being "*torn*" in two. Sound familiar? The only other time Mark uses *schizo*, the Greek word for "torn," is in Mark 1:10, when God tears the heavens open. While everyone is questioning where God is, He's working where we aren't looking. He's in the temple *tearing* the curtain to the holy of holies because a new and living way to Him is being made through the death of His Son. He's very much at work, more than

He's ever been. The indicator is there: He's tearing. He's just not where we are expecting, nor where we are looking.

In both instances where the word "torn" is used by Mark, it is used in a passive construction. This means the doer of the action is not revealed. He's hidden. God reveals Himself through His work, but *He* remains hidden in the process. Do you still need to be convinced that God is out there in the darkness? There's more.

Suddenly, a voice speaks up.

> *And when the centurion, who stood facing him, saw that in this way he breathed his last, **he said, "Truly this man was the Son of God!"*** (Mark 15:39)

A wink?

Oh, yes. It's a centurion. And he calls Jesus *"the Son of God."* This is precisely what the Father called Jesus during His baptism and transfiguration. Coincidence? No. Paradox? You guessed it. Centurions were detested by the Jews. They were foul and violent, the last people you'd expect to call Jesus the Son of God. In fact, Roman centurions called only Caesar the son of god. Yet, this centurion has a conversion experience at the cross and switches his allegiance to Christ.

Was the Father at work? More than ever. And His words are the same, only where you'd least expect to find them: on the lips of a centurion. You'd have missed them if you were waiting for them to thunder from heaven.

And so, we see, the Father did not abandon the Son. He was there the whole time, working where we might least expect Him, doing something far deeper and greater than anticipated.

If you're wondering where He is, though you may not see Him at work, you can assume He's doing far more than what you're supposing. He's out there, somewhere in the mystery. Alive in the night sky.

There's no controlling the Creator. There's no putting Him in a jar. Instead of offering oversimplified answers about the way God works, the way this story is told suggests that we can't predict what God is doing or where He will show up next. This deters us from making sweeping statements about what God may or may not be doing. Instead, it exhorts us to trust in a God who evades our answers but requires our faith.

When the sky turns ominous, when the darkness is so thick that you feel it swallow you while you wonder where God is, you might not need an answer. You just need to trust God enough to keep your eyes open. A flicker of light might just wink when and where you least expect it.

Wink #5

GOD WINKS IN OUR DOUBTS

An old adage says, "Starve your doubts." I'm not on board with this one. It suggests that doubt can't serve *any* purpose, but I believe doubt can be helpful.

While doubt isn't the end in and of itself—for nobody has a goal of being a doubter—doubt *can* be a means to the end, which is trusting God more deeply. That being the case, we shouldn't dismiss our doubts, rebuke them, or command them to vanish because they cause a little bit of suffering. We should pay attention to them. Work through them. Give them a place and see what they are saying. God may just wink in them.

The longer I walk along the journey of faith, the more it becomes apparent to me that doubt is an elemental part of the process. Doubt is like the ache in my feet that stops me in my tracks when I'm on a long hike. I must stop and deal with the ache. And I'm given an opportunity to see something I may have missed or wasn't searching for to begin with. A bird feeding its young. A deer trotting along a fence. A father pulling his daughter in a wagon.

Let me offer a better example. One of the best days I ever had was a Thursday I spent ambling around Paris in 2014. I had a few days to myself while working in Italy for the summer. I flew to the City of Love to see *all* the sights—the Louvre, Notre Dame, the Champs-Élysées, the Arc de Triomphe, and, of course, the Eiffel Tower. From 8:00 a.m. until 7:00 p.m., I didn't stop a single time except to have a croissant. Then, I was back on the go, certain I would see it all, certain I *was* seeing it all. I must have walked over fifteen miles.

Somewhere around seven in the evening, my body could take it no longer. It demanded rest. At this point, I was no longer in charge. The arches in my agonized feet were calling the shots. I had to pause and honor my aching extremities. After buying a soda and a baguette, I took a seat near the Eiffel Tower. Only then did I see something I hadn't planned to see.

Near the steps of the Place du Trocadéro, dozens of couples in love were dancing. Wrapped in embraces, they swayed to the sound of a street band led by an accordion. Mesmerized, I watched for over an hour with eyes that rarely blinked. This display of spontaneous romance left an impression on me that the famed places I had come to see had not. I thought I knew all the sights. I hadn't. That evening, my aching arches winked at me. They slowed me down. I honored what was aching me. This created an opportunity to *really* get to know the City of Love.

Do we ever become so preoccupied with finding what we think we ought to know that we despise our doubts for slowing us down—like the aches in our feet—and, to our detriment, miss the things we ought to see, things that appear only when we give attention to what is hurting us? I think so. In our doubts, God is saying, "Look. There's something here I want you to see." Most of the time, it's something we didn't even know to search for.

OFTEN, WHEN OUR DOUBTS SLOW US DOWN, GOD IS SAYING, "LOOK. THERE'S SOMETHING HERE I WANT YOU TO SEE."

John's gospel gives the picture of a man with his doubts—an individual who must deal with what's aching him—"Thomas the Doubter" or "Doubting Thomas," as he's called by some in the pejorative sense. Yet, the way John sketches the character of Thomas is a bit different from the unbeliever we mistake him to be. In rethinking his doubt, we catch a wink.

To see this wink, we must first consider why John writes his gospel. He was evangelizing Jews and Jewish proselytes who were expecting the Messiah. (See John 20:31.) He wants his audience to arrive at the conclusion that Jesus is God. So, John begins the story saying, *"In the beginning was the Word, and the Word was with God, and the Word was God"* (John 1:1). Jesus, known as the Word, is God. John starts the story with his goal in mind. From here until the end, he knits each detail within the narrative to support this point. This includes how he develops his characters, particularly how things shake out with Thomas.

In John 20:24–29, Thomas takes the center stage. The first thing we are told about Thomas is that he is not with the disciples when Jesus appeared to them for the first time after His resurrection (verse 24). We aren't told where he is. We don't know what he was doing. John leaves it to our imagination. All we know is that Thomas *isn't* present. He could be out gallivanting. He's somewhere on his own, doing who knows what.

The disciples later tell Thomas that they saw the Lord. Thomas says, *"Unless I see in his hands the mark of the nails, and place my finger into the mark of the nails, and place my hand into his side, I will never believe"* (verse 25). Thomas's refusal to believe comes off strongly in the Greek, for it uses *ou mē* after the future or subjunctive mood, which is the strongest form of negation. It could be translated, "In no way at all will I ever believe!"

It's waggish how John continues the story. Although Thomas is adamant that he will not believe Jesus has risen, in the very next verse, John shows Thomas with the rest of the disciples the following Sunday. (See John 20:26.) Did he think the Lord would show up? Maybe not. It's doubtful.

But stop for a second and consider: Thomas *was* there with the other disciples. This suggests he *was* wrestling with his doubts. On the outside, he was adamant he wouldn't believe, but something deeper was going on within. He was wrestling. And to Thomas's credit, he honored that ache in his soul. He gave pause. He stopped his Sunday wandering. And to his surprise, he ended up seeing the Lord.

It's important to recognize how Jesus handles Thomas's doubt. He doesn't say, "Ya know, Tom, I don't know what to do with you. Come on. How many times did I tell you I was going to rise from the grave? And you didn't believe Me. The rest of My disciples did. But you? What's wrong with you, ya doubter?"

Instead, Jesus treats Thomas's doubt as legitimate. He offers Thomas an invitation to know Him more profoundly, saying, *"Put your finger here, and see my hands; and put out your hand, and place it in my side"* (verse 27). Jesus *uses* Thomas's doubt as the means to make him a stronger, more thorough believer.

Thomas's response? *"My Lord and my God!"* (John 20:28). This happens to be what John said about Jesus in his very first verse. By exploring his doubt, Thomas achieves what John was hoping his audience would gain after reading his gospel. This is the wink from Scripture. Thomas nails it.

It portrays Thomas as an ideal disciple. He is not the unbeliever we think he is. He is an example of what a disciple should be. A doubter? Yes. A believer? All the more. Disciples are those who use their doubts to know God deeper and trust Him more completely. In the early church, those who were uncertain about Christ would have been encouraged after reading this. Like Thomas, they, too, could use their doubt to come toward Christ and discover who He is.

Thomas's example tells us that the road to faith is often paved by doubt. It may seem that God's great men and women are *at all times* people of faith. But a careful examination of their stories shows that these individuals have *moments* of great faith amid a lifetime shadowed by doubts.

Those who know God the deepest are those who have doubted the hardest. Job doubted God's goodness. (See all of the book of Job.) Gideon doubted God's ability to help him win the war against the Midianites. (See Judges 6.) While he was in prison, John the Baptist doubted whether Jesus was the Messiah. (See Luke 7:18–20.) Elijah doubted that God would protect him from the wicked Jezebel. (See 1 Kings 19:1–3.) Though the list goes on, there is enough here to show that deep doubts can pave the way for you to *really* know the Lord and have a deeper understanding of who He is. Thomas's conclusion, *"My Lord and my God!"* winks at us. It assures us of this.

Are you suffering with profound doubt? Now is the moment to give pause. It's time to honor what is aching you. Explore it. See where it takes you. The doubt that is wrenching your soul will direct your eyes toward the luminous Christ. When you see what you ought to see, you'll say, *"My Lord and my God!"* And God will wink at you...through your doubt.

Wink #6

GOD WINKS IN THE RED HERRINGS

God isn't usually up to what we think He's up to. At least, I can speak for myself and say that's the case. *When I'm most certain, I am most certain to be wrong.*

He's a clever God who escapes our suspicions. The moment you suspect *this*, God does *that*. If you suspect *that* because you've learned He won't do *this*, God does *something else.*

As He told the prophet Isaiah:

> *My thoughts are not your thoughts, neither are your ways my ways...For as the heavens are higher than the earth, so are my ways higher than your ways and my thoughts than your thoughts.* (Isaiah 55:8–9)

God's providence surprises us. He has more modes of operation than we have guesses. He's not sneaky or scheming. He's just *not obvious*, especially in times of suffering. It's a subtle thing.

An obvious God would be convenient. We would prefer a God we can probe, one who allows us to compute and anticipate His actions. But God resists our computations because *He* is the One who computes the whole universe. He watches our ways and knows our thoughts from afar. (See Psalm 139:2.) *If it were the other way around, we'd be God and He'd be our creation.*

God will never let it be so. May *we* never think it's so. Imagine worshipping a god you've created, one whose actions you can predict because you have formularized his ways. Worshipping a god that follows *our* script is the essence of idolatry and a prescription for tedium. Boredom would set in. You could no longer respect and obey him. Your wonderment would cease.

No. *We are made to be enchanted by God.*

Just when we become sure of what God is doing, God winks. Everything we were certain He was doing turns out to be a red herring. We realize, *Yes, that's it. That's God at work.*

In literature, a red herring is a false clue or misleading hint that distracts readers from the matter at hand. Those who pick up on a red herring become distracted from what's *really* going on in the plot and go down the wrong path. The term was popularized by the nineteenth century journalist William Cobbett, who used a smelly fish to distract hounds that were chasing a rabbit. In this study, I use the term "red herring" to mean a misconception.

How often does our own estimation of God's ways turn out to be a red herring? How often do we believe that *this* person is "the one" who will end our loneliness? That *this* presidential election will fix the country's suffering? That *this* job will solve all financial woes? That surely *this* is the explanation for someone's pain? Then the relationship ends in heartache, the country keeps on suffering, the job falls through, and the person's pain worsens.

Our certainty was the smell of fish.

But providence winks when we're following a red herring. Even though our thinking has gone off track, God has not. He hasn't stopped working even if our suspicions were faulty and let us down.

There's something thrilling about providence. It has its own surprising script for suffering. I'm relieved that there is more in motion than my own conceptions—and misconceptions. God lets me sniff around over here and over there, kind of like a Christian Sherlock Holmes. When I am disappointed by what I find, I'll later learn that God's been up to more. *He's not limited to my delusions because He's not a creation of my comprehension.* That's enchanting.

John's gospel is filled with characters who follow a red herring. They are on the wrong scent and have mistaken notions. Whatever they think is right is wrong. There's not a Sherlock Holmes, Hercule Poirot, or Nancy Drew in the bunch. For the most part, they don't have a clue regarding Jesus's identity—not even His disciples. Sure, they know who He is—their teacher. But not who He *is*.

They have their own perceptions—ideas they seem to be certain about. John brings those perceptions to the forefront to warn us of our own that we believe to be correct. We should always be careful to avoid careless certainty when it comes to matters of the divine.

> ## WE SHOULD ALWAYS BE CAREFUL TO AVOID CARELESS CERTAINTY WHEN IT COMES TO MATTERS OF THE DIVINE.

The first character to examine is the Samaritan woman whom Jesus meets at the well. (See John 4:7.) After her encounter with Jesus, she rushes back to her town to tell everyone, *"Come, see a man who told me all that I ever did"* (4:29). In her estimation, Jesus is simply *"a man."* Seems a bit ordinary. A modest review. What's the big deal?

It gets interesting when we examine the next character. In John 5:5–7, we meet an invalid who has been crippled for thirty-eight years. After healing him, Jesus says, *"Get up, take up your bed, and* walk" (verse 8). When the Jews chastise the former invalid for carrying his bed on the Sabbath, he says, "*The man who healed me, that man said to me, 'Take up your bed, and walk'*" (verse 11).

Here is another person who refers to Jesus simply as a *man*. What's going on here?

It's not that Jesus wasn't a man. He was 100 percent Man. John is making a point to show that many of those around Jesus are certain He's *just a man*.

In John 7, we see this again. The chief priests and the Pharisees send the temple police to arrest Jesus, but they halt their effort and return. Why didn't they follow orders? The police reply, "*No one ever spoke like this man!*" (verse 46). Here is yet another sure conclusion that Jesus is only a man.

The story continues. In John 9:1–7, Jesus heals an individual who was born blind. The Pharisees are upset and talk among themselves.

> Some of the Pharisees said, "*This man is not from God, for he does not keep the Sabbath.*" But others said, "*How can a man who is a sinner do such signs?*" And there was a division among them.　　　　　　　　　　　(John 9:16)

The Pharisees might not know exactly who Jesus is, but one thing they are sure of is that He's *only* a man.

From there, we find a more explicit reference in John 10. Pious Jews gather around Jesus with the intent to stone Him during the Feast of Dedication. Jesus asks why. They reply, "*It is not for a good work that we are going to stone you but for blasphemy, because you, being a man, make yourself God*" (verse 33). The pious Jews are certain He is a man pretending to be God and deserves to be stoned. It's interesting how certain the pious always seem to be.

Later, in John 11:47, the chief priests and Pharisees gather the Sanhedrin to decide how to deal with Jesus, who had just raised

Lazarus from the dead. They say, "*What are we to do? For this **man** performs many signs.*" Caiaphas suggests that Jesus die as a scape-goat on behalf of the nation. He says, "*It is better for you that one **man** should die for the people, not that the whole nation should perish*" (verse 50). The faction that represented God had God in their midst, and they didn't notice. They were sure He was *just* a man.

During the trial of Jesus, a servant girl approaches Peter and says, "*You also are not one of this **man's** disciples, are you?*" (John 18:17). Meanwhile, Jesus is led to Pilate's house, and Pilate asks, "*What accusation do you bring against this **man**?*" (verse 29). Both the servant girl and the governor—the lower class and the ruling class—are sure they see *just a man*.

Things come to a head in John 19:5. Jesus has just been flogged, and Pilate presents Him to the people. He is swollen and bruised; His flesh is torn open. He is wearing a crown of thorns and a purple robe. The whole sight is a mockery, both cruel and vicious. Pilate exclaims, "*Behold the **man**!*" The people jeer and cheer. They demand that the Man they hate so much be crucified. So certain He is a man, so unaware that He is God.

The Scripture winks at us. It tells us something the characters don't.

Remember now, in the first verse of his gospel, John states that Jesus is God, "*In the beginning was the Word, and the Word was with God, and the Word was God*" (1:1).

Toward the end of his gospel, John states:

> *Jesus did many other signs in the presence of the disciples, which are not written in this book; but these are written so that you may believe that Jesus is the Christ, **the Son of God**, and that by believing you may have life in his name.*
>
> (John 20:30–31)

John begins and ends his gospel with a statement that Jesus is God. The irony is that, in between, there are characters who can't seem to tell. As certain as they are about everything, they don't notice at all.

John has set it up this way. God is doing something beyond their line of reasoning, outside of their sureness, all while He is at the well or near the pool. Healing eyes or raising the dead—He's working on the behalf of those with misconceptions. They think Jesus is solving the problem of suffering one way, but He's going to do it another way. The Word made flesh. The Lamb of God. He's headed to the cross to take away their sins and conquer the evil behind their misery. And the sure and certain folks don't see that because they are following a red herring.

LIKE THE CHARACTERS IN THE GOSPEL OF JOHN, WE MAY BE FOLLOWING A RED HERRING AND MISSING THE VERY THING GOD IS DOING RIGHT IN FRONT OF OUR FACES.

The elements of the story serve as a subtle wink to those of us who think we know it all. It cautions us that we, like the characters in the Gospel of John, may be following the red herring. It's a gesture in our direction. It signals that we can miss the very thing God is doing right in front of our faces.

Are you certain about something you think God is doing to solve your woes or the woes of the world? Are you sure about it? Although you may be wrong, there's good news. God's providence doesn't stop working just because you're mistaken. He winks while you're following the red herring, and He continues to work.

Jesus went to the cross on behalf of all those who thought He was *just a man*. He still worked on their behalf. He did it despite their misconceptions. If you can be sure of anything, you can be sure He'll do the same for you.

Wink #7

GOD WINKS IN OUR HINDSIGHT

I have mixed feelings about looking at old photos. Once or twice a year, I take a look at them and remember who I used to be. I examine old hairstyles. I squint at shoes I used to love. Sometimes, I chuckle at the things I'm doing—things I no longer think are cool. *Who is this guy? He looks familiar. Is that really me?* I deliberate and determine that although I am the guy in those photos, he's not the same person I saw in the mirror this morning—to my relief.

I enjoy examining the process of my becoming. As a spiritual man, I notice the grace of God in my development, a grace that has shaped me during times of suffering. I notice it now, far more than I did back then. This must be because grace in suffering is not easily seen with nearsighted eyes. When we are too close to the moment, it seems it isn't there, or perhaps it's just a blur. The further removed we are from the moment, the clearer it becomes that God's grace has been present and working all along the way.

For instance, I see a picture of myself on a beach in a foreign land more than a decade ago. I am holding two fish. The sunburn on my skin and the smile on my face cover the sadness in my heart. I was a broke, struggling pastor wondering if I had anything worthwhile to say. I suffered in a different way back then. My anxiety was louder than any rationale: *Nobody wants to come to your church. You should have studied to be a surgeon. You'd have more money.* I lived those days in fear. I felt my life was ruined before it had started. I was timid and afraid about my future. I used a nighttime cold medicine to put myself to sleep almost every night.

I look at this photo today, and God winks in my hindsight. I have different thoughts: *God's grace brought me to that beach. God's grace gave me the opportunity to catch those two fish. God's grace ended up carrying me from that beach to almost fifty other countries. That was only the beginning of something great.* Within the chaos of my fear, God was alive in the darkness and forming me. His grace was at work in my pain, although I only noticed this later in hindsight.

An interesting account in Scripture illustrates how God's grace works through suffering in the process of our formation. It's found in John's gospel in the unfolding of the character Nicodemus.

Nicodemus was an interesting fellow. His name means "conqueror of the people," a fitting title. He was a Pharisee who was part of the ruling class in Judea. (See John 3:1.) It's safe to presume he was part of the Sanhedrin and likely a prominent figure within the group. In fact, he is so prominent that Jesus calls him "*the teacher of Israel*" (3:10). For Nicodemus, in Greek, the article of par excellence is used in front of "teacher." This suggests that Nicodemus was *the* teacher in Israel. Nobody else was on his level.

Nicodemus pops up in the story at a few different points. After introducing him in 3:1, John says Nicodemus "*came to Jesus by night*" (3:2). His decision to come to Jesus at night was perhaps to be secretive, out of fear that he could be seen. During this meeting, he and Jesus dialogue about being born again. Nicodemus doesn't get what Jesus is talking about, nor does he understand who Jesus is. (See John 3:2–21.)

There is double entendre in his coming to Jesus *"by night."* On one hand, it is literal. On the other hand, it is not. Nicodemus *himself* is in darkness. He is a sinner, and his understanding is veiled. (See verse 19.) The dialogue ends, and Nicodemus remains in the dark.

We don't notice God's grace at work in Nicodemus's life. It's too soon in the story to observe God forming his life in the darkness and shaping him into what he'll become.

But the story moves ahead. Nicodemus pops back up again, a slightly different man. This time, we have hindsight to compare.

It is about six months before Jesus's crucifixion. The chief priests and Pharisees are talking about arresting Jesus. Nicodemus, being one of them, defends Jesus. (See John 7:50–52.) He suggests that they ought to give Jesus a fair trial. The Pharisees don't like his suggestion and accuse him of being one of Jesus's followers. Notice any difference in Nicodemus? He has dealt with his fear. His empathy for Jesus is not a secret anymore. He's now defending Jesus openly, in front of those who want to kill Him. God's grace has grown in Nicodemus's life. He's a little bolder than before. Has God been working on Nicodemus, the man who suffered with fear in the night? The text is winking.

The third and last time we see Nicodemus is after Jesus's crucifixion in chapter 19. We've gained even *more* hindsight, and we see that he's even *more* transformed than in chapter 7. Here, Nicodemus comes to anoint the body of Jesus with a large quantity of spices.

Cleverly, John drops a hint. He reminds readers this is the same Nicodemus *"who earlier had come to Jesus by night"* (John 19:39). Why would John think it so important to include *this* detail about Nicodemus at this point in the story? The Scripture winks at us again.

It's because he *is* different. Nicodemus is tending the body of Jesus, who was tried as a criminal and accused of insurrection. This was a serious offense. It could get any of Jesus's associates into trouble. But Nicodemus doesn't care. God's grace has been at work in the darkness, and now Nicodemus's understanding is no longer blinded about who Jesus is. No longer a man of the night, Nicodemus isn't the blind, timid Pharisee he used to be. He's a courageous follower of the Lord, tending to Christ in the open. He is now in the light.

The way John unfolds the story of Nicodemus illustrates to us a bit about our own becoming. God often forms us in the night as we suffer alone with what plagues us and the things we fear. But rest assured, His grace is at work. It may not be apparent in the moment, but when we look back at the whole narrative, we begin to see the picture. The picture tells us that God has been using our suffering to shape us. If we didn't notice, it's because we've been too nearsighted to tell.

Consider your own life for a moment. Who do you perceive in the mirror today? Do you see a doubter? Someone with shame? Maybe a fair evaluation suggests that you aren't a good mother or that you're a negligent father. It could be that you are an unfaithful boyfriend or a jealous girlfriend. It can be dark facing who you are. It produces suffering of a different sort.

GOD CAN FORM YOU IN THE DARKNESS
AND DRAW YOU OUT OF THE NIGHT,
JUST AS HE DID NICODEMUS.

But time will go by. The person you see today doesn't have to be the person you see tomorrow. Between the spaces of time, God's grace works. God can form you in the darkness and draw you out of the night, just as He did Nicodemus. You may not notice this happening. It may take a decade for you to finally look back and see God wink through your hindsight. But that doesn't mean that God isn't at work. In fact, who's to say He's not at work right now while you read this book? Maybe the fact that you're reading this sentence is God winking in your direction. There's more going on in your night season than you can imagine.

I used to have mixed feelings about looking at old photos. I don't anymore. Old photos provide an opportunity to observe the process of my becoming what God's grace has enabled me to be. They afford me an occasion to count who I was and to see who I am no longer. They encourage me that who I am today is not who I will be tomorrow. They give me courage to face the night I am in today and to know God's grace was once at work...and *is* still at work.

Though I am too nearsighted to see it right now, tomorrow I'll see God wink. And so shall you.

Wink #8

GOD WINKS IN OUR PERCEIVING

When we wrestle with the uncertainties of life, we wrestle with the identity of God. A healthy consideration of God is always under adjustment. Events unfold. Time transpires. Suffering goes unresolved. We stand on the seashore, stare into the blackness, and face the mystery. We soon discover that our conceptions of God—often misconceptions—call for a revision. A vigorous faith amends its perception of God when it must.

How we grow in our awareness of God can be likened to birdwatching. Most birdwatching seems to take place when one is sitting in the rain without a bird in sight. The birdwatcher waits patiently. Suddenly, an orchard oriole flies into view. The birdwatcher is familiar with this bird. She's seen it before. Only this time, she notices the slight curve of its beak. Odd, she hadn't noticed this in the past. In her recollection, its beak is straight. She makes a scribble in her notebook and amends what she once supposed. It's a short encounter, mere seconds. But the birdwatcher's understanding is enhanced for a lifetime. Ironically, the bird is still a mystery. Plenty remains to be discovered. The birdwatcher will be back tomorrow.

Coming to know God is a similar process. Life can be dreary, especially when suffering abounds. We wait out most of it, with no view of God in sight. *Will we see Him again? Perhaps He isn't in this forest?* Suddenly, God explodes into sight. There's something about Him we hadn't noticed before. It's different than what we thought we knew. It changes what we had once believed. It leaves an impression on our soul. It transforms our perception. We see suffering in a new light. There's hope. We know God a bit differently now, a bit better. Yet there's still much to be discovered. We'll be back tomorrow.

Perceiving God is illustrated for us in John chapter 9. It's a moment when Jesus lands on a branch for a birdwatcher to see. The texts wink. There are improvements to be made in our perception of the divine. It will affect how we perceive suffering. Scribbles will be made in our notebook.

John introduces to us *"a man blind from birth"* (9:1). His blindness is symbolic. It illustrates humanity's inability to perceive the Lord on our terms. We see the Lord when He reveals Himself to us. He makes Himself known when He so chooses. In the midst of our sorrow and suffering, God determines when He will burst onto the scene and land on the branch. We can trust His timing is right.

The story moves along. Jesus heals the man. (See John 9:6–7.) The most important element in the story is not the healing itself. John's focus is on the reaction of the people toward the healing and how the man responds to those who inquire.

The man's neighbors, those who knew him as a blind beggar, ask about his healing. He tells them:

> *The man called Jesus made mud and anointed my eyes and said to me, "Go to Siloam and wash." So I went and washed and received my sight.* (John 9:11)

It's important to note how the man refers to Jesus the first time around. He calls Jesus a *man*. It's his initial observation, his first perception. This little detail often escapes our attention. However, it's significant.

The Pharisees make the second inquiry into the man's healing. They ask him what he thinks of Jesus. He replies, *"He is a prophet"* (verse 17). Notice, he doesn't refer to Jesus as a man; instead, he attributes more to Jesus this time around. Now he considers Jesus a spokesman for God. Is he seeing more than he had? Is his perception being amended? A scribble is made in his notebook.

The Pharisees are so baffled that they go to his parents and ask them what happened to their son. The parents tell the Pharisees they don't know. They tell the Pharisees they should ask their son because he is old enough to speak for himself. (See John 9:18–23.)

So, once again, the Pharisees question the man. They ask him how Jesus opened his eyes. They were dumbfounded and perplexed because healing was rare in the Old Testament. It happened only in extreme instances. (See, for example, 1 Kings 13:4–6.)

The man who had been blind since birth tells the Pharisees, *"If this man were not from God, he could do nothing"* (John 9:33). Here, he attributes even more to Jesus. Now, Jesus is a man sent from God. Another scribble in his notebook. He makes an adjustment.

The story goes on. Jesus appears to the man He had healed and asks, *"Do you believe in the Son of Man?"* (John 9:35).

> *He answered, "And who is he, sir, that I may believe in him?"*
> *Jesus said to him, "You have seen him, and it is he who is*
> *speaking to you." He said, "Lord, I believe," and he worshiped*
> *him.* (John 9:36–38)

Notice, he calls Jesus "Lord." He's gone from calling Jesus a man, to calling him prophet, to calling him one sent from God, and finally to worshipping him as Lord. His perceptions have continued to change throughout the narrative. He has decided what John wanted his readers to acknowledge: Jesus is God. (See John 1:1.)

The Scripture winks at us. It tells us there is a process at work. All the details are not observed in one instance. It took time for the man born blind to reach his conclusion. There can be no hurry in discovering God.

IT TOOK TIME FOR THE MAN BORN
BLIND TO REACH HIS CONCLUSION THAT
JESUS IS LORD. THERE CAN BE NO
HURRY IN DISCOVERING GOD.

Like the man, we, too, continually adjust our perceptions of God. This is healthy, rigorous faith. With each adjustment, the Lord becomes more exalted, and our view of Him grows more profound.

The man's conclusion ends with worship. Our observations will lead us toward worship. Even in times of suffering, our scribbles will cause us to bow our knees and say, "Lord, I trust in Your goodness. What I know today gives me more reason to have hope in You for tomorrow." When our perceptions are refreshed, our worship is revived.

Remember that everything you seem to know about the Lord is not actually the case. I have learned to write more in pencil than pen. The very things we count on are the very things liable to change.

We saw this with the pandemic. Those certain that God would not allow it to last longer than a few months realized—quickly—that this wasn't the case. Those who assumed the spoken word would drive it away found that God doesn't always respond to our commands. Those sure the clergy were immune had to say goodbye to many of its fallen. Some overlooked this.

But many of us found ourselves sitting in the woods on a rainy day, hoping for a bird to show up on a branch and wink at us in our suffering. We wrote down scribbles. We adjusted our perceptions.

Our faith came alive. Our worship was revived. We can confirm that God is still good. We can trust Him. We will come back tomorrow to look for Him, waiting to discover more of what we don't know, especially when mystery blindsides us.

Wink #9

GOD WINKS IN OUR UNCERTAINTIES

Uncertainty is part of the journey of faith. Though not a virtue, uncertainty is inevitable terrain for a disciple of Christ. We must tread, unsure of where it leads. We don't *need* to know, and that's a hard thing to accept. It's difficult to let go of certainty. It's comfortable in our hands.

When we relinquish our need for certainty, we can take hold of the Master. He's the certain One in times of suffering. He takes us along the unfamiliar way. At times, He opens our eyes. We see. We are assured for a moment. We know that wherever the Master is taking us is good. He winks; He's at work. And then we go back to being uncertain again. We venture into the unknown, letting Him lead the way. We need the Master all the more. This is faith: trusting in God to lead us through a mysterious life where suffering abounds.

Mark gives us a picture of this in his gospel. Throughout the narrative, we see that Jesus's disciples are walking the terrain of uncertainty. They don't quite realize who Jesus is. They don't ever grasp the significance of what He does. (See Mark 6:51–52.) They struggle to make sense of what Jesus means when He speaks. (See Mark 8:15–19.) And even though Christians today know the narrative's direction is headed toward the cross, the disciples could never imagine such suffering ahead. (See Mark 8:31–32.)

Mark doesn't put the disciples' uncertainty on display to encourage us to be uncertain. Yet it does suggest that uncertainty is part of following Christ in this world that teems with sorrow. As He leads, we will often find ourselves unsure, even mistaken. Such uncertainty has not disqualified us from following. It gives us all the more reason to follow Him.

In Mark 8, we find a story that winks to us in our uncertainty. It is an unusual story that often perplexes readers. Jesus is again working with a blind man.

> He took the blind man by the hand and led him out of the village, and when he had spit on his eyes and laid his hands on him, he asked him, "Do you see anything?" And he looked up and said, "I see people, but they look like trees, walking." Then Jesus laid his hands on his eyes again; and he opened his eyes, his sight was restored, and he saw everything clearly.
>
> (Mark 8:23–25)

What's the deal with the Jesus's first prayer? Did He have a bad day? Was His healing power rusty? Perhaps it was some side effect to His healing virtue? It seems strange to think that Jesus, who is God, prayed for a man to see, only to have the man get blurry vision instead.

I've heard explanations for this verse that are less than satisfying. One is that the blind man's faith was feeble. Another is that it sometimes takes two or three attempts to pray for a person before they receive their healing. I think these conclusions come from looking at this healing story apart from the grander story of Mark's gospel, the larger whole of what is going on.

When we look at this story as part of the whole, we'll notice this account of healing is another intercalation:

+ Part I: The disciples are uncertain (Mark 8:14–21)

  » *Intercalation:* A blind man sees trees walking (Mark 8:22–26)

+ Part II: The disciples experience a moment of certainty (Mark 8:27–30)

In Mark 8:15, Jesus tells His disciples, *"Beware of the leaven of the Pharisees and the leaven of Herod"*—and then they talk about only having one loaf of bread to eat. Jesus rebukes them and says, *"Do you not yet perceive or understand? Are your hearts hardened?"* (verse 17). They are uncertain. Yet, in Mark 8:27–30, a moment of clarity comes: Peter, on behalf of the disciples, correctly answers Jesus about who He is. (See verse 29.) The story of the man being healed of blindness (8:22–26) comes between these accounts.

LIKE THE BLIND MAN WHO SAW PEOPLE AS TREES WALKING, THE DISCIPLES WERE MOVING FROM BLINDNESS TO PERCEPTION, UNCERTAINTY TO CLARITY.

The Scripture winks. Like the blind man, the disciples couldn't see. They were blind and didn't know who Christ was. Then, like the blind man who saw people as trees walking, they get a small glimpse of who Christ is, though perceiving Him in a blur. Later, when Christ rises from the dead, they see clearly who He is. (See Mark 16.) They were moving from blindness to perception, uncertainty to clarity. I think Jesus was illustrating this process to them in the way He healed the blind man.

Look at what happens in Mark 8:31–33. Jesus tells His disciples that He must suffer, be killed, *"and after three days rise again"* (verse 31). Peter gets upset at Jesus for saying this and begins to rebuke the Master. Peter is blind again. It is literally a moment of certainty, stifled by the mention of suffering. He's back to being uncertain about what His master is doing, challenged with the prospect of a life that abounds with suffering. Jesus gives him a rebuke for this. (See Mark 8:33.) Peter will wrestle with Christ's suffering the rest of the way through Mark's account. (See Mark 14:66–72.) He will find himself challenged to let go of his need to be in control and follow Christ, despite the sorrow he's uncertain about.

Discipleship is a battle with uncertainty that never comes to a complete end in this life. As disciples, we must tread this terrain while we trust the One directing our lives. At times, we are blind and uncertain; at other times, our vision is fuzzy and blurred. But one day, when Christ comes to reign, all things will be clear. Until then, can we venture into the unknown and trust God to lead us in this mysterious, sorrow-filled life where it's hard to see?

While we can now perceive who Jesus is because of the work of the Spirit (see Acts 2), I don't think that means we will always be certain of everything God is doing in our lives. We still find ourselves in the narrative of Mark, relating to the disciples' oblivion. Most of the time, we can't seem to figure out what the Lord is up to in our suffering. We guess wrong. We are without a good clue. Then, there are times when our eyes catch a blurry picture of what the Master is doing. From that blur, we're able to make out a wink that encourages us. We rediscover Him again as the Sovereign of our lives. But then we go back to being uncertain. And so, we must trust and have faith for Him to lead us in the mystery.

There will be a day when we know the work of the Master most clearly. Like the blind man, so too will our eyes be totally healed. In that day, we look back and our eyes will behold the path He has been walking us down all along. But until then, we will *see things imperfectly, like puzzling reflections in a mirror* (1 Corinthians 13:12 NLT).

Despite this, we can hope for winks in this journey of discipleship—moments when our vision is clear enough to glimpse the good Master we have been following through the uncertainties of this uncertain life.

Wink #10

GOD WINKS IN OUR THEOLOGY OF SUFFERING

What role does the suffering, with all its mystery and complexity, play in your theology? How well have you integrated it into your way of life? I ask this question because much of pop Christianity avoids suffering, preferring subjects that seem more overtly triumphant. Have you noticed how much Christian literature and media is devoted to ways of managing a successful business, finding the right spouse, and crafting the body that can make you happy? For many, personal satisfaction seems to be the goal.

I get uneasy when our theology of suffering is swept under the rug. In many respects, I think we have failed to see the mystery of suffering as part of our faith. It has become what we avoid—an enemy to vibrant faith—even though Jesus explained that suffering is an inevitable aspect of following Him and is necessary for triumph. (See John 16:33.) You can't overcome without it. If we don't wrestle with suffering in the text, we aren't reading Scripture the way the gospel writers intended. Our idea of triumph will be twisted. We will overlook where God is and what He is doing. And that's a problem.

Keith Warrington, a Pentecostal theologian, believes that the theology of suffering needs to be restored. He says, "The recognition of the place of suffering in Pentecostal theology needs to be redeemed as an integral aspect of an authentic spirituality that acknowledges the value of suffering in the life of the believer and does not simply attempt to exclude it or assume that its presence is intrinsically illegitimate."[4]

He suggests this in relation to Pentecostal churches specifically because Pentecostals have a robust theology of healing. From out of their denominations have come alternative movements, such as the word of faith movement, which emphasizes prosperity, health, and success. It's not uncommon for suffering to get circumvented in these movements or for its leaders to offer a truncated theology of suffering.

LUKE 24 IS ONE OF THE MOST IRONIC CHAPTERS IN THE ENTIRE NEW TESTAMENT. IT INFORMS US THAT TRIUMPH COMES THROUGH SUFFERING.

One Scripture passage that can help to redeem the theology of suffering is found in Luke 24. Here we find one of the most ironic chapters in the entire New Testament. It winks at us and informs us that triumph doesn't come by avoiding suffering; it comes *through* suffering. It encourages us to integrate suffering into our theology and, ultimately, into how we practice our faith.

In verse 13, we find two disciples walking to the village of Emmaus. Jesus has risen from the dead, but these two are unaware of this. As they are walking, they discuss the events that surrounded Jesus's death. Suddenly, the resurrected Jesus approaches them and joins their walk. The two do not recognize Him. (See

---

4. Keith Warrington, *Pentecostal Theology: A Theology of Encounter* (New York, NY: T&T Clark, 2008), 303.

verse 16.) One is named Cleopas, whom the historian Eusebius believed was the brother of Joseph, Jesus's foster father.

Jesus asks them what they are talking about. Cleopas asks, *"Are you the only visitor to Jerusalem who does not know the things that have happened in these days?"* (verse 18). Jesus asks him what he's talking about. And they reply:

> *Concerning Jesus of Nazareth, a man who was a prophet mighty in deed and word before God and all the people, and how our chief priests and rulers delivered him up to be condemned to death, and crucified him. But we had hoped that he was the one to redeem Israel.* (Luke 24:19–21)

This is where the Scripture winks at us.

Here in the last chapter of Luke, the two men are disappointed because they *think* Jesus has failed to redeem Israel. The irony comes into play. In the first chapter of Luke, Zechariah prophesies that God was at work redeeming Israel through the events leading to Christ's birth: *"Blessed be the Lord God of Israel, for he has visited and redeemed his people"* (verse 68).

Later, in chapter 2, Luke tells us about a prophetess named Anna who meets the baby Jesus in the temple. Anna's response reiterates the theme of Christ as Redeemer to those who were present. *"She began to give thanks to God and to speak of [Jesus] to all who were waiting for the redemption of Jerusalem"* (Luke 2:38).

As readers, we expect to see Christ fulfill His redemptive work by the time Luke's gospel ends. Yet instead, we meet Cleopas and his friend who say it isn't so. Could this be a twist in the story? Did Christ fail to redeem? Their hasty assumption is irony and comes off humorously. It is a wink, an *aha* moment.

The two individuals who are so certain they are right are instead deeply wrong. Certainty can be such an enemy to discipleship! They had a false expectation of redemption. Their heart was set on a national military triumph. They assumed that the Messiah would overcome politically through a crushing conquest. Suffering wasn't part of the equation of triumph.

Jesus tells them they are *"slow of heart"* for this misunderstanding and introduces His theology of suffering, saying, *"Was it not necessary that the Christ should suffer these things and enter into his glory?"* (Luke 24:25–26). Jesus is clear: triumph requires suffering. Never in their wildest imagination could they expect the Messiah's victory to come this way. Their theology was all wrong. The place that suffering has in conquest escapes them as it does in much of pop Christianity. According to the way of Jesus, glory and suffering are inseparable. A failure to see this is a misunderstanding about the Christian faith and eventually leads to disappointment.

The next thing Jesus does is interesting. He explains suffering to them by interpreting the Old Testament Scriptures. *"And beginning with Moses and all the Prophets, he interpreted to them in all the Scriptures the things concerning himself"* (Luke 24:27).

MEETING TWO DISCIPLES ON THE ROAD TO EMMAUS AFTER HIS RESURRECTION, JESUS INTERPRETS SCRIPTURE FOR THEM THROUGH THE LENS OF SUFFERING.

The word "interpreted" comes from the Greek word *ermēneuō.* It is also where we get the word "hermeneutics," which refers to the interpretation of Scripture. The Lord interprets Scripture through the lens of suffering. If we fail to see Scripture through this lens, then we aren't reading it like the Lord. We won't know what it means to conquer. Our ideas of victory will be twisted. The apostle Paul would agree. He says, *"For I consider the sufferings of this present time are not worth comparing with the glory that is to be revealed to us"* (Romans 8:18). Suffering and glory go hand in hand. If we suffer, we will also reign with Him. (See 2 Timothy 2:12.)

This was part of Christ's hermeneutics and theology. This was part of His apostles' doctrine—and it must be part of ours.

Luke 24 winks at us. It insinuates that suffering has a central place in our Christian lives, mysterious as it is. Just because we don't understand it and don't like it doesn't mean it should be swept under the rug. It shouldn't be something we only concern ourselves with when there is a pandemic or disaster. Instead, we must regularly consider suffering in the way we interpret Scripture and the way we practice our faith. That's not to say that we can't have ambitions of biblical success or desire to be prosperous. However, even the prosperous and successful will suffer explicitly. And they will know others who suffer.

We should consider it now; otherwise, we'll truncate it later. Do you have a theology that works when things don't appear triumphant by the world's standard of triumph? A theology like this is mysterious...and very, very subtle. But it is a theology like Christ's. In it, we discover a God wink.

Wink #11

GOD WINKS IN OUR WAY OF SUFFERING

Suffering is the way of Christ. This statement can disturb us; it prods our flesh and makes us feel uncomfortable. No one likes to suffer. Who wants to imagine that sorrow is an essential component of the faith we have chosen, the faith by which we order our lives? The terrain of discipleship might be more difficult than we thought. Did you sign up with suffering in mind?

To clarify what I mean by suffering, I am referring to the cost of following the way of Jesus. Christian suffering means rejection, persecution, and a separation from the status quo. It can be a disorienting sense of estrangement that prevents us from the comfort of fitting in. There's a Japanese saying appropriate for this: "The nail that sticks out gets hammered back in."

The way of Jesus is so subversive to the systems of society that a Jesus follower is certain to be noticed and, at some point, pounded with spite—especially if they live in a society with a distaste for Christianity. For this reason, Jesus calls it the "narrow gate" (Matthew 7:13). He was saying that few would choose this fate for themselves. But the Scripture winks. It illustrates that as we traverse this way, we discover Christ. We experience His glory when we experience the way of His suffering. When we share in Christ's sufferings, we are closest to Him, united with Him in a profound way. Where is God? Along the way of suffering.

WHEN WE SHARE IN CHRIST'S SUFFERINGS, WE ARE CLOSEST TO HIM, UNITED WITH HIM IN A PROFOUND WAY.

Those who have suffered the most for Christ seem to be the best acquainted with Him. Their affection for Jesus stirs up a holy envy in me. The way they speak about Christ differs from what I'm used to hearing and how I'm accustomed to speaking. It's as if they've met Him and have been hanging out with Him. It's often said in our church circles, "Come to this conference and you'll meet Christ" or "Listen to a sermon each day and you will know Him better."

Yes, there's a certain knowledge you'll come to know about Jesus from feeding off the Word. But to know Him the way He was known (see Isaiah 53), we must experience His struggle with the world. Do we really want to be with Christ? It takes more than a conference or a podcast. It takes more than seminary. We must suffer. (See Philippians 3:10.)

Where is God while you suffer? Perhaps the better question is, "Where are you?" You have joined Him in His way.

I think of my dear friend, a full-time pastor in Vietnam. For several decades, he has served God's people in the communist land.[5] I've had the opportunity to visit him and be among his family and congregation in Vietnam on several occasions. In 1991, he was arrested for preaching the gospel. He was imprisoned for

---

5. The story of his imprisonment is told in DC Talk's *Jesus Freaks: Stories of Those Who Stood for Jesus, the Ultimate Jesus Freaks* (Bloomington, MN: Bethany House Publishers, 1999), 238–240.

more than a year. He spent time in solitary confinement in a hole in the ground just large enough for his body to squeeze into. I've heard him describe the nightmare more than once. My nerves can hardly stand it. Despite his great suffering, he shared Jesus with the inmates by writing Scriptures on cigarette paper and tucking the paper away in a pen that got passed from cell to cell.

His experience is not without effect. It's penetrating when he speaks of Jesus. He articulates the gospel with divine conviction. It's as if Jesus was speaking. In his own suffering, my friend has joined the Master. This is the road of glory.

In the Gospel of Mark, the Scripture winks and shows us that suffering with Jesus is the way to glory—how to know Him most intimately. In Mark 10:32, Jesus and the disciples are on their way to Jerusalem. Two disciples, the brothers James and John, approach Jesus and make a request. They perceive this procession to Jerusalem as a march to magnificence and a path to splendor. In their estimation, Jesus is headed to take political power. This is where He would be glorified, they imagine. They don't want to miss out. They want to join in on His reign. They say to Jesus, *"Grant us to sit, one at your right hand and one at your left, in your glory"* (verse 37). In Jewish custom, these were the highest positions of honor. They want to secure a place of authority in Christ's kingdom. It's a selfish request. They imagine glory without suffering.

For them, conquest was the way to glory. Following Jesus meant political triumph. Their assumption is ironic because Jesus had told them this wouldn't be so. Prior to this, on several occasions, He informed them that suffering, not conquest, awaited Him in Jerusalem. (See Mark 8:31; 9:31; also Matthew 16:21; 17:22–23.) Perhaps they had selective hearing. Or maybe they thought they knew better than Jesus. Be that as it may, suffering wasn't part of their plan. But why should it be? The Roman Empire was built on conquest. Society valued strength and power. They couldn't imagine glory any other way.

Jesus tells James and John that they do not know what they are asking. Their idea of how He will achieve glory is all mixed up. Jesus informs them that they will suffer like Him because they follow Him. (See Mark 10:39–40.)

As the narrative moves forward, Jesus goes into Jerusalem. Here He is crucified as He said He would be. There is a unique scene in here that Mark is careful to record. The subtle language he uses calls us back to Mark 10:37, where James and John requested to sit on either side of Jesus. This is where the Scripture winks at us. It tells us that Jesus's real moment of glory was not found in a political triumph, but at the height of His suffering and His death.

Mark 15:27 points out that two criminals are crucified with Jesus, *"one on his right and one on his left."* Ironic, isn't it? To be at Jesus's right hand and left hand in His glory means to join Him in His suffering and in His death. It's being crucified with Him and dying the death He died. It is fellowship with His suffering.

GLORY IS NOT FOUND ON A THRONE IN A PALACE; IT IS FOUND ON A CROSS AT CALVARY. THIS IS THE SUBVERSIVE WAY OF JESUS.

Glory is not found on a throne in a palace; it is found on a cross at Calvary. This is the subversive way of Jesus. While the rest of the world vies for glory through conquest, the follower of Christ yields to the suffering of his Master. Where is God today? He's near the suffering. That is where He's found, and where He winks.

As followers of Christ, it's important to recognize the place of suffering. We must count it as a valid and necessary part of our journey of faith. We shouldn't try to escape it because to do so would forfeit His glory.

You may never be called to give your life, like the disciples did. Chances are you'll never go to prison like my friend the Vietnamese pastor.

But you will, at least, experience rejection, disorientation, or discomfort for doing things the way of Jesus. See it as an opportunity to join Christ and count it as an occasion to know Him more profoundly. These experiences will grow your faith in ways that sermons, devotionals, conferences, and even this book cannot. When you suffer for the cause of Christ, He will wink at you. And in this wink, you will know Him in ways you never could otherwise. We should consider this mystery in our distress.

Wink #12

GOD WINKS IN THE ACTS

Glory in suffering is an element of discipleship. We observe this throughout the duration of the New Testament. We see it first in the Gospels, demonstrated in the life of Christ. But it doesn't end with the Messiah.

As the biblical narrative moves along, Luke brings the notion to life by presenting it in the lives of the apostles. It is central to Luke's theology—so central that he weaves it throughout the entire book of Acts. Luke leaves no room for readers to expect otherwise. A disciple of Christ reads the narrative and gets a hint of what's ahead. In the way of Christ, suffering comes before glory. How puzzling. How perplexing. Yet, the story in Acts winks and tells us this is so.

The first wink Luke uses to inform us is his name for Christianity: *"the Way"* (Acts 9:2; see also 18:25; 19:9, 23; 22:4; 24:14, 22.) His subtle metaphor continues the entire story of Acts, portraying the Christian disciple on a journey. It is a difficult journey, filled with challenges, sorrow, and distress along the way. Amid these come great demonstrations of God's power and salvation. Luke's readers come to expect their own road of discipleship to look the same, with both suffering and glory for God.

A more vivid picture of "the Way" comes into focus as Luke traces the journey of the apostle Paul. When we first meet him, he's "*a young man named Saul*" (Acts 7:58) who's present at Stephen's execution. Stephen was one of the seven men chosen by the apostles to serve tables and ends up being the first Christian martyr. (See Acts 6:1–5; 7:54–60.) Prior to his death, Stephen appears before the Sanhedrin and gives a lengthy discourse that serves as a testimony to the risen Christ. After he is stoned to death, Stephen is portrayed as a suffering witness who enters into glory.

In Acts 8:1, we're told, "*Saul approved of* [Stephen's] *execution.*" This is a wink. The way Luke sets up the story depicts Stephen passing the suffering witness baton to Paul. From this point forward, Paul will suffer for Jesus as we follow him along the Way. When we get to the end of the story and find Paul in prison for Christ, guess who receives the baton? You guessed it—you and me.

As the story moves on from chapter 8, Luke employs another literary device to develop the idea of glory in suffering. He parallels the ministry of Paul to the ministry of Christ, subtly painting them with the same brush by bringing the similarities of their experiences into line.

LUKE PARALLELS THE MINISTRY OF PAUL TO THE MINISTRY OF CHRIST, SUBTLY PAINTING THEM WITH THE SAME BRUSH BY BRINGING THE SIMILARITIES OF THEIR EXPERIENCES INTO LINE.

First, we notice that both Jesus and Paul are on a journey, headed toward a particular destination where they will suffer for their witness. Jesus is headed to Jerusalem, where He will die. (See Luke 9:51; 13:22; 17:11; 18:31–33; 19:28.) Paul is headed to Rome where he, too, will die. (See Acts 19:21; 23:11; 27:24.)

Next, in Acts 21, Paul is arrested by the Romans, and the crowd shouts, "*Away with him!*" (verse 36). In Acts 22, this same language comes from the tribunal after Paul gives a speech and testifies of Christ. They say, *"Away with such a fellow from the earth!"* (verse 22). This *"away with"* phrase is related to language Luke uses in his gospel when Jesus was on trial and the crowd condemned Him: *"But they all cried together, 'Away with this man, and release to us Barabbas'"* (Luke 23:18). This suggests that Paul was suffering like his Lord. (See Acts 9:16.) They were on the same journey.

Third, Luke confirms that both Jesus and Paul are innocent sufferers. The whole of Acts 21–28 portrays the innocence of Paul as does Luke's account of Jesus. (See Luke 23:47.)

These analogous details are not coincidences. Luke has intentionally written them in this manner. It's a subtle wink to us. As we conclude the story, we realize that if our ministry will parallel Christ's and the apostle Paul's, there's likely suffering ahead. We are challenged to follow Paul in the Way, just as he followed Christ.

When I was in seminary, I wrestled with this. My dorm mates and I were discussing a chapel service we had attended. The speaker's emphasis was focused on *what's in it for me.* He made subtle yet repeated references to his expensive possessions. Some of the students had dollar signs in their eyes.

One classmate's Christian formation had been centered on similar teaching. She would always tell me how God was blessing her. Some of the stories, I'll admit, seemed far-fetched. Once she told me she had made a large sum of money at her job, which seemed like a hefty payout for a college student. My initial thought was that it didn't make sense, yet I had no reason to be suspicious.

While discussing the chapel speaker's sermon in the dorm, my friend emphasized his displeasure, noting, "It's not a cross-shaped gospel." He then went on to tell us about a woman in one of his classes who followed this teaching. She admitted that she had been making up lies about how God was at work in her life. I knew who he was talking about. It all made sense. "She says she tells people these things because it brings glory to God," he said.

Her idea of the Way was wrong. Her idea of where God is and what He is doing was much the same as the world's. God is not found in material possessions, wealth, and the best things that money can buy. That is not the Way of Christ. It's not the road Luke describes in Acts. To the world's surprise, God is in the suffering and the struggles, He's alive in the trial, and He's near those who bear reproach for His name.

GOD IS NOT FOUND IN MATERIAL POSSESSIONS, WEALTH, AND THE BEST THINGS THAT MONEY CAN BUY. THAT IS NOT THE WAY OF CHRIST.

The glory that Paul and the other disciples experience along the Way in Acts—union with God (Acts 7:59–60), healing (9:32–35), direction from the Holy Spirit (16:6–10), miraculous deliverances (16:25–27), and supernatural rescues (27:23–44)—occurs in their times of suffering and great sorrow.

This is the irony of the Acts of the Apostles. Glory is wedded to Christian suffering. The chapel speaker and the young woman classmate hadn't made this connection.

It's an easy mistake to make in our culture. Any of us could make it. Christianity has become inundated with materialism and Western ways of measuring success. The story of Acts winks. It calls us back to the Way of Christ—to understand discipleship the way the apostles did, to be with God where we don't want to go.

Let us remember what Paul said when looking back on his cross-shaped journey:

But he [Jesus] said to me, "My grace is sufficient for you, for my power is made perfect in weakness." Therefore I will boast all the more gladly of my weaknesses, so that the power of

Christ may rest upon me. For the sake of Christ, then, I am content with weaknesses, insults, hardships, persecutions, and calamities. For when I am weak, then I am strong.

(2 Corinthians 12:9–10)

Glory in suffering and power in weakness are part of the mysterious way of the kingdom. *Where is God?* Just examine the story of Acts. Does it look like your story? If so, your life parallels Christ's. And He's not far off.

Wink #13

GOD WINKS IN OUR DISCIPLESHIP

Power. Miracles. Signs. Wonders. If you've been in charismatic or Pentecostal circles, you may have heard it said, "These follow those who follow Christ." I agree. We should expect demonstrations of God's Spirit to accompany our obedience as Christ's disciples.

The expectation doesn't stop there. We should expect suffering, too. To expect one without the other is problematic. Where is God? God is at work in the healing *and* He's at work in the beating. He's at work in the curing *and* He's at work in the crushing.

In my doctoral thesis, I examined how early Pentecostal disciples thought and wrote about suffering for the first thirteen years of their movement, from 1906 through 1919. The first ten years of a movement represents its heart and values; I extended my studies to include the conclusion of World War I in 1918 and the Spanish Flu pandemic, as these were trying times in which the early Pentecostal movement endured.

I was fascinated to discover that early Pentecostals suffered immensely. They were often the victims of harassment, which included bullying, property damage, bodily injury, and verbal abuse. (This is not to say that other Christians have not suffered immeasurably. They have and still do.)

A. J. Tomlinson, the first general overseer of the Church of God in Cleveland, Tennessee, had bullets shot through the window of his home. F. F. Bosworth, an early Pentecostal pioneer and delegate to the first General Council of the Assemblies of God in 1914, was severely beaten by twenty-five men. C. H. Mason, co-founder of the Church of God in Christ (COGIC), was jailed in Lexington, Mississippi, for ostensibly preaching against the war as well as his interracial convictions and practices. Early Pentecostal publications such as *The Apostolic Faith*, *The Bridegroom's Messenger*, and the *Church of God Evangel* are filled with stories and testimonies of missionaries suffering and dying on the mission field.

What surprised me the most during my research was their attitude toward this suffering. It can best be summed up by a quote from a 1919 issue of *Church of God Evangel*, edited and published by Tomlinson. In his full front-page article entitled "The Blood of Lost Souls Will Fall Upon Somebody. Will it be You?" he writes:

> Let the folks work and make the money and living that cannot preach, and have no ability or talent for it. But those who have ought to go into it [ministry] and stick to their job if they die in their tracks of starvation. Go into it boys, if God has chosen you and sent you in His great harvest field; then obey the call, and if He lets you suffer and die of starvation then die at your post. Be a hero for God. Stand hard things, and don't be afraid. Stick to your job or else don't claim the call.[6]

The early Pentecostals didn't run from the suffering caused by persecution. More than that, they weren't angered by the notion that God might not deliver them. As disciples of Christ, they

---

6. A. J. Tomlinson, *Church of God Evangel* vol. 10 no. 5, February 1, 1919; accessed via pentecostalarchives.org.

knew God was in their suffering. He was alive in the darkness of their chaos, mysteriously working all things together for their good, even if they lost their lives. They saw their affliction as an opportunity to be "a hero for God."

> THE EARLY PENTECOSTALS DIDN'T RUN FROM THE SUFFERING CAUSED BY PERSECUTION. THEY SAW THEIR AFFLICTION AS AN OPPORTUNITY TO BE "A HERO FOR GOD."

Imagine a pastor telling his congregation that a victorious Christian life is enduring persecution and dying for God on the mission field, having to daily overcome harassment with love, or accepting the role as the wildly unpopular person in their social spheres. My suspicion is that the church would gain few new members the following Sunday.

I don't think it's too far off to say that our perceptions of victorious Christian discipleship have been sedated by a culture that values certainty, security, and power. What God is doing better not tip the apple cart! We seek control and comfort, believing God's in what we can control, what puts us at ease, and what gives us a sense of might and power, like miracles.

Do our ideas about discipleship match the early Pentecostals, or are they a fanciful daydream with no humiliation and distress?

Jesus might have noticed His disciples' notions about following Him turning into a daydream after having sent them out to heal the sick and deliver the broken from demonic powers. (See Mark 6:7.) All that power. All those miracles. What's next? In their thinking, Jesus was going to overthrow the Romans and set up His own kingdom as a political autocrat. They'd reign with Him, of course. Why wouldn't they? They *were* His disciples after all. Disciples share in their master's glory. They thought, *God is in the power. He's in the miracles! Next, we reign.* Ah, the life.

But wait—not so fast. Suffering precedes glory. It's the mysterious way of the kingdom. God is near to the sufferer. We cannot work the works of God without hardship.

The way Mark tells the story emphasizes this. He does so in a brilliant yet subtle way that's difficult to notice until someone points it out. Then you can't miss it. To execute this, Mark uses another intercalation that yields a pleasant surprise. It winks in our direction.

We find this in Mark 6:7–13, when the twelve apostles are sent out by Jesus to do miracles. Afterward, they come back to Jesus to report all that they had done and taught. (See verses 30–31.) Power. Miracles. Victory. Things were going great.

One moment before we jump the gun.

In my experience, this story in the Gospel of Mark is often told with just verses 7–13 and 30–31. Verses 14–29 are usually left out and are not perceived as part of the story. These *seem* like an awkwardly placed story about John the Baptist's fateful doom in being put to death by Herod. *But* that's the truly subtle irony. It *is* part of the way Mark tells the story. When we include it in the narrative, the intercalation looks like this:

+ Part I: Jesus sends out His disciples with power to heal (6:7–13)

  » Intercalation: John the Baptist is put to death by Herod (6:14–29)

+ Part II: The disciples come back and report to Jesus all that they had seen (6:30–31)

That John the Baptist's death is placed between the sending out and the coming in of the disciples is a suggestive wink in our direction concerning the nature of discipleship. It's communicating what's often missed for following Christ.

Until the sending of the Twelve, John the Baptist was the major voice of proclamation for the kingdom. Then he was killed and went off the scene. The disciples were coming on. The baton was being passed to them. The insertion of John the Baptist's death right smack in the center of their commission would indicate to the disciples—and all those seeking to follow Jesus—that persecution and suffering come with being a disciple. The intercalation winks at us and tells us that the disciples could expect the sufferings of John the Baptist. Perhaps Mark used an intercalation to sneak this into the story as an ironic way of showing how easy it is to overlook the prospect of suffering when we follow Christ and do His miraculous work.

Regardless, the disciples would reign with Christ in His kingdom. (See Romans 8:18–19.) But not until they suffered. To think otherwise is a daydream. The world is not so friendly toward those who are part of the kingdom. Anyone desiring to be a disciple of Jesus should know this before deciding to follow.

We should accept suffering the way the early Pentecostals did and heed Mark's wink. This wink is an invitation for us to realign the way we think about discipleship—to accept our suffering as a way of knowing Christ as He was during His earthly ministry.

The early Pentecostal theologian E. T. Slaybaugh proposed this. He noted there were three degrees of knowing Christ based on Philippians 3:10: knowing Him as our Savior from sin; knowing Him through Spirit baptism; and knowing Him in His sufferings. To this, he said:

> Many people who have entered into the two former experiences with Christ fail to grasp and enter into the truth, reality and blessedness of his sufferings. It is the entering into the latter experience with Christ, in addition to the two former, that makes one "conformable unto His death," out of which comes the transformation into His

image, which transformation qualifies one for the first res-urrection from among the dead…to become a part of the Bride.[7]

As disciples, what will our attitude be toward our suffering? When our suffering feels like uncertain chaos, we can trust that God is at work in that chaos, using it to transform us. We come to know Him and be like Him.

What was meant for evil, God means for our good. God is at work in the healing, and He's at work in the beating. He's at work in the curing, and He's at work in the crushing.

Be a disciple. Be a hero for God.

7. E. T. Slaybaugh, "Jesus Is Coming Soon," *The Bridegroom's Messenger*, April 1, 1913, p. 4; accessed via pentecostalarchives.org.

Wink #14

GOD WINKS IN THE CROWD

It takes great courage to trust Jesus and follow Him in times of suffering and uncertainty. This was certainly in the case in the first century. There was *great* suffering during the time of Christ, especially among the Jews. The Romans oppressed the Jewish people by forcing them to pay taxes to Rome and follow Roman laws. This led to political unrest, which led to apocalyptic tensions.

Messianic expectations were high. Would a deliverer come to save the Jews from their tribulation and sorrow? The grand narrative of the gospel is set to this background of sorrow and uncertainty. It posed the questions, "Is Jesus the Messiah? And who will trust in Him as such?"

These questions are asked of us today, in our own times of sorrow and uncertainty. Can we trust the Lord when we see millions suffering under oppressive governments? Is Jesus the Messiah even though the world is always under threat of nuclear incineration? Is Jesus working in our midst despite our human frailty when dealing with viral outbreaks, tsunamis, and other calamities? Will we trust Him as such? How will we behave in the face of these real situations?

Scripture exhorts us to trust the Lord in this life of suffering and uncertainty by giving us examples of individuals who meet Jesus. We discover those with great faith who seem to believe that Jesus is the Messiah and trust Him, such as the Roman centurion who believed that Jesus could heal his servant from a distance with just a word (see Luke 7:1–10) and the Canaanite woman who knew He could free her daughter from demonic possession. (See Matthew 15:21–28.) We also find examples of those who don't seem to know He's the Messiah or who have the wrong expectations of Jesus and *don't* trust Him as such—like the disciples, surprisingly.

These characters provide windows that enable us to examine our own lives. We are supposed to differentiate the good examples from the bad and yearn to be like the good, which can help us react to suffering with the right frame of mind. Which character in the text will we exemplify amidst uncertain distress?

IN MARK'S GOSPEL, "THE CROWD" IS PORTRAYED AS A SINGLE CHARACTER THAT'S IMPULSIVE AND UNRELIABLE.

In Mark's gospel, Mark winks at us and tells us who *not* to be: the crowd. The crowd is portrayed as a single character in Mark. It maintains one personality and acts as a single unit. Jesus meets the crowd at almost every turn. An analysis of how Mark portrays those in the crowd gives us a lot to reflect on.

We first meet the crowd in chapter 2. Jesus is in a home preaching to the people inside as well as those standing outside. Four men come to Jesus carrying a paralytic, hoping Jesus might heal him. (See Mark 2:1–5.) We know the story. They lower the man down to Jesus from the roof above. Why didn't they just go in through the front door? *"They could not get near him* [Jesus] *because of the crowd"* (verse 4). The first thing that Mark suggests about the crowd is that they were preventing someone who was suffering from seeing Jesus.

In chapter 5, Mark again tells us about a troublesome crowd. Here, we meet a woman who's suffered with an issue of blood for twelve years. To touch Jesus's garments, she has to fight her way past *"a great crowd* [that] *followed him and thronged about him"* (Mark 5:24; also see verses 27, 31). Again, the crowd is preventing an afflicted person from seeing the Lord.

Mark's characterization of the crowd is a wink. If we want to see how God *can* work and *is* at work in suffering, we must push back at the crowd.

Mark continues characterizing the crowd in chapter 6. Here, the crowd is compared to lost sheep with no direction of their own. (See verse 34.) They are fickle, *"For many were coming and going"* (verse 31). The crowd's fickleness plays out as the rest of Mark unfolds. Slowly, they turn against Jesus. Although Jesus taught them, healed them, and fed them twice (see Mark 6:30–44; Mark 8:1–21), they sell Him out. In Mark 15:11, the crowd is swayed by the chief priests. The last thing we hear of the crowd is their wish to crucify the Lord. (See Mark 15:13–15.) The crowd is capricious, impulsive, and unreliable.

Mark is winking in our direction. *Don't be like the crowd!* The crowd walks away from the Lord in times of suffering.

The crowd, the masses, the throng, the mob—call it what you will, it is the way of the world. Mark shows us that the crowd's way prevents us from seeing Christ in times of suffering *and* even *turns its back on Christ* when suffering begins!

This gives us pause to consider: When crises present themselves to our world, do we get caught up in the way of the crowd? Are we fickle?

Take the COVID-19 pandemic. What was the crowd doing during this? Mass hysteria. Fearmongering. Panic. Hate.

Exclusion and marginalization. Conspiracy. Everyone for themselves. Blaming God. Those in churches weren't unaffected by this attitude.

Is this how we are to handle uncertainty? If it is, we will miss what God can do…and *is* doing. We won't see it. We may even get angry at the Lord. We could assume He's not "there." We ask, "Where is God?" and all the while, we are following the masses.

WHEN SUFFERING TAKES PLACE, INSTEAD OF PANICKING OR ACTING HYSTERICALLY, WE SHOULD GO AGAINST THE CROWD AND PLACE OUR HOPE IN THE LORD.

When suffering takes place, devastating as it might be, our hope should be in the Lord. Instead of panicking or acting hysterically, we should go against the crowd by considering, "How is Jesus at work in this suffering? How can I put my trust in Him? How will I keep from abandoning Him?" Doing this will get us close to the Lord to observe something He's doing. And He'll wink.

It is my observation that the pandemic has taught us a little something about following the crowd versus trusting Jesus as Messiah. I once asked my church, "How many of you regret any of your past actions during this pandemic—be it a post on social media, a conversation you had, or a temperament you lived with?" Almost every hand went up, including my own.

Hindsight proved that many of our responses to the suffering were crowd-like. They were fickle, knee-jerk reactions produced by emotion, selfishness, fear, or even following politically charged talking points. The crowd was definitely *not* trusting the Messiah.

We must push at the crowd if want to be near Jesus and see Him at work in suffering. In Mark 7, Jesus heals a man who is deaf and has a speech impediment—but first, He takes the man "*aside from the crowd privately"* (verse 33). There's something powerful in this verse. If we want to hear the Lord, trust the Lord, and experience His power in our suffering, it requires separation from what the masses do, think, and speak.

The next time there is great suffering in our world or in your own personal life, separate yourself from the way the masses believe and behave. When you find yourself engulfed by the crowd, push back. You'll see God wink.

Wink #15

GOD WINKS IN IMMANUEL

Suffering abounds. God's presence abounds more. This is a theme found throughout Scripture. God is in the midst of evil, working despite the evil. We don't always know why evil happens, but we do find God's presence despite it.

God *wants* us to discover His presence. For the here and now, His presence *is* the answer.

In the Gospel of Matthew, we find the world in great turmoil. We are instantly met with one of the greatest forms of suffering that could be imagined: infanticide, the practice of killing unwanted children soon after birth. I can't think of anything more inexplicable than the suffering of an innocent child.

Remember Andrea Yates? She was the Texas mother who murdered her five children, ranging from six months to seven years old, by drowning them in a bathtub in June 2001. Her case shocked the nation.

Yet archaeologists have discovered that infanticide was a common practice in the Roman world. In Matthew 2, we are introduced to the mad king Herod, who was concerned that the birth of the Messiah would threaten his reign. Out of jealousy, the crazed king ordered the death of all male children two years old and younger in Bethlehem and around the region. (See verse 16.) Infanticide.

Did you know this is part of the Christmas story?

We tend to overlook this verse. In my own experience, I've rarely seen a pause for reflection about the massacre of the innocents during a velvet rendering of the Christmas story. Who wants to discuss this horrifying event before they open up Christmas presents and try Grandma's cookies? That is why I'd like to call attention to it now.

When we read Matthew 2, we cannot help but ask, "Why would God allow such psychotic evil to persist?" We are given no answer. All we get is one verse. How odd. It's mysterious. We find a major atrocity and all we get is one verse, with no explanation. The Scriptures don't seem to be the least concerned about *explaining why* God would allow it. It would have been nice for Matthew to drop us a footnote that included his theodicy. But he does not.

THE GOSPEL OF MATTHEW FOCUSES ON IMMANUEL, "GOD WITH US." THIS SUBTLE INCLUSIO FRAMES THE ENTIRE BOOK.

Yet the story *does* speak to horrendous events such as infanticide. But it gives us hope amid such evil. How? The focus of the story is Immanuel, God with us.

This is how Jesus is first introduced. Before the infanticide, an angel appears to Joseph and tells him that the baby in Mary's womb *"will save his people from their sins"* (Matthew 1:21) and is to be called Jesus. Matthew says this fulfilled Isaiah's prophecy: *"'Behold, the virgin shall conceive and bear a son, and they shall call his name Immanuel' (which means, God with us)"* (verse 23). The first thing that we are told about Jesus in the entire New Testament is that He is *"God with us."*

This is vital. It is Matthew's wink to us that amid mankind's great suffering, God will be present. He is with us in the suffering, executing His plan. Within that plan, He became the sufferer Himself. While the narrative again tells us nothing about *why* God has allowed the infanticide to persist, we are told that Jesus has entered into the world where it occurs, and He suffers a similar unjust death.

God with us...in the suffering. *God with us*...in the infanticide. God's presence near us...in unjust death.

This is where Matthew's theology of suffering begins, and it's also where it ends. Matthew gives a wink in the last verse of his gospel that God is still with us in our troubles.

Jesus tells His disciples, who watched Jesus suffer and who would suffer like Him, *"And behold, I am with you always, to the end of the age"* (Matthew 28:20). Isn't it interesting that the first thing Matthew tells us about Jesus is that He is *"God with us"* and the last thing we discover about Jesus is that He is *always* with us. He entered our suffering, and He remains with us in our suffering. The disciples would come to find this out in their own unjust deaths.

God being *"with us"* is a subtle *inclusio* that frames the entire book of Matthew. Unlike an intercalation, where a seemingly unrelated story breaks up the narrative, an inclusio is a word or phrase that *frames* in the narrative. In other words, the narrative begins and ends with the same word or phrase, emphasizing the content in the middle.

It looks like this:

+ *"God with us"* (Matthew 1:23)

   » The events of Matthew's gospel

+ God with us *"always"* (Matthew 28:20)

The Scripture winks at us. It tells us that, amid the sufferings and sorrows of life—despite genocides, infanticides, pandemics, and human agony—the Creator is here. He is actively at work. He is Immanuel. He isn't far off. He has not forgotten us. He drank the cup of our humanity. And He's somewhere in the middle of this. Not knowing *why* doesn't change that.

French theologian Suzanne de Dietrich said:

> The history of the People of God is all strewn with blood and tears…The rage of man is unfurled upon the Elect of God…Our own time has seen massacres equally shameless. The testimony of the evangelist [Matthew] is that God nonetheless pursues the purpose of salvation.[8]

We make a hasty assumption that the purpose of Scripture is to give us all the answers. By now, you know that it is not. Rather, the Word shows us the nearness of God who, as de Dietrich suggests, is involved in our salvation from inexplicable sorrow.

Can we readjust our focus as we read Scripture? Is it possible to take the energy we spend asking *why* and redistribute it toward discovering what Jesus is up to now and how He is at work as Immanuel? That Jesus is here and at work is later evidenced in the lives of the apostles.

Take Stephen, for instance. When he was stoned for following Christ, he saw Immanuel near to him. (See Acts 7:56.) When Paul was shipwrecked, Immanuel stood by him in the presence of an angel. (See Acts 27:23.) Even as he neared his death, Paul affirmed God's nearness and faithfulness. (See 2 Timothy 4:17–18.)

In all this, we never find an explanation, only the presence of God, with us in this. If you wonder why, you are in good company. You are like the rest of those who have followed Christ through the ages. God's people have been tortured, imprisoned, mocked,

---

8. Suzanne De Dietrich, *The Gospel According to St. Matthew* (London, UK: John Knox Press, 1961) in Leon Morris, *The Gospel According to Matthew* (Grand Rapids, MI: William B. Eerdman's Publishing Company, 1992), 45.

flogged, stoned, stabbed, and even sawed in half (see Hebrews 11:36–37) with no explanation before their deaths.

But God never failed to make His presence known during their suffering. He is Immanuel, *"God with us,"* and He winks to let us know He's there.

Wink #16

GOD WINKS IN OUR FAILURES

God's presence is Christ's faithfulness. In times of suffering, we can expect to see Christ's devotion to us. This is a promise for us as disciples. Jesus is faithful to those who follow Him. But what happens when we fail as followers?

One way we suffer as humans is through our own failures. These aren't demonic attacks or horrific actions such as infanticide that happen outside of our control. They are the pain we bring upon ourselves because of our own frailty and brokenness. It results from our sin. This may include the consequences of our dysfunction—like patterns of behavior that cause us to repeatedly hurt other people or our self-talk that dissuades us from trusting Christ and being obedient to Him.

Can you think of some of your own ways that have caused you to fail the Lord more than once or twice, even repeatedly? We all can. Despite our failures, the Scriptures wink.

While the goal of being a disciple is being faithful to the Master, the irony is that following Christ has more to do with Jesus's faithfulness to us than our faithfulness to Him. Yes, we need to strive to be faithful. However, even our own faithfulness is a result of His faithfulness to us. When we fail and suffer for it, He remains with us.

Matthew winks at us and demonstrates this explicitly in his gospel. Perhaps the most ironic thing is that the disciples rarely get it right in the story. The disciples fail so often that their example is one the reader should *not* follow. We should *not* be like them if we want to follow Jesus.

But Matthew gives us subtle clues that show us that the mission of the disciples is never compromised, despite all of their failures, because Jesus remained faithful to them.

THE MISSION OF THE DISCIPLES IS NEVER COMPROMISED, DESPITE ALL OF THEIR FAILURES, BECAUSE JESUS REMAINED FAITHFUL TO THEM.

The wink is found in the strange number of times that Matthew refers to Jesus's disciples as *"his disciples."* Matthew does this twenty-four times. (See Matthew 5:1; 8:23; 9:11, 19, 37; 10:1; 11:1; 12:1, 49; 13:36; 15:23, 32; 16:13, 21, 24; 19:23; 23:1; 24:1; 26:1, 36; 27:64; 28:7, 8, 13.) This might seem to be unintentional but given the failure of the disciples throughout the narrative, it's likely not. It's precise irony. Those who are "his" can't get it right.

This is even more absurd when we consider that Jesus empowers them for service. (See Matthew 10:1, 5–15.) He gives them power to cast out demons, heal the sick, and receive supernatural provisions for their needs. Yet, they don't know how to feed the multitudes when Jesus tells them to (14:16–17; 15:33), they can't cast out a demon from a possessed boy (17:16), they are frightened by a storm (14:22–33), and they fail to understand who Christ is (16:21–23). Humorously, the only thing *"his disciples"* do get right is retrieving a donkey (21:6–7). This is Matthew amusingly suggesting that they are good only for mundane tasks. Some disciples they are!

But despite their disappointing failures woven into the narrative, they are confirmed as His disciples. Placed in their failures, this sounds like an affirmation. It is a reassurance that no matter how badly they nosedive, no matter how much pain the failures cause them, no matter how much suffering, Jesus never walks away. He never stops shepherding them. He never turns His back on them in search of more competent disciples. He remains loyal amid the trouble they cause for themselves. He stands committed to them until they get it right.

In last chapter of Matthew, "*Mary Magdalene and the other Mary*" visit the tomb of Jesus (Matthew 28:1). Except for John, the disciples have once again failed Jesus by abandoning Him in the hour of His crucifixion. Of all their disasters, this was the worst. They proved to be cowards. They let Jesus suffer on His own.

When the women get to the tomb, an angel appears to them, concerned about the disciples who have failed Jesus. He tells the women, "*Go quickly and tell **his** disciples that he has risen from the dead*" (verse 7). So they "*ran to tell **his** disciples*" (verse 8).

In their most severe failure, the disciples are reaffirmed. They are still "*his.*" God is still with them. He is still at work in them. Though they can't see it or feel it because of their failings, Christ is still near. They are His.

Jesus appears to the women while they are on the way to tell His disciples that the Lord has risen. He tells them, "*Go and tell my brothers to go to Galilee, and there they will see me*" (verse 10). Jesus calls them His "*brothers.*" This is significant. Though the disciples have failed Jesus in a major way, the faithful Jesus acts as though the relationship has never been interrupted. This defies any rational explanation, outside of the divine loyalty of Jesus towards His own.

Finally, in the last verse of this gospel, the Lord tells them, "*Behold, I am with you always*" (Matthew 28:20). He promises them His never-ending faithfulness as they take up their mission. It's as if He said, "Don't worry. I know there are times you will fail. But your success as disciples has never been based on your own success. It has been based on My presence. As you go, I will be here. And because of this, you will fulfill My will."

Matthew's gospel heralds this. Count on the presence of Christ despite our brokenness. We will have failures along the way, and they will cause us pain and suffering. Our failures may hurt others as well. This does not disqualify us as followers of Christ. Rather, it tells us how much we need the Lord.

OUR FAILURES DO NOT DISQUALIFY US AS FOLLOWERS OF CHRIST. RATHER, THEY TELL US HOW MUCH WE NEED THE LORD.

As a pastor, I've come to see this candidly, not only in my own life, but in the lives of those I have shepherded. I have seen people in the flock make decisions with huge consequences, and yet through it all, the Lord never abandons them to their suffering. In His faithfulness, He restores the individual. He leads them back the way they are called to walk. Is there pain? Of course. Is there suffering? Plenty of it. Is there grace? Even more so.

I think of a person who attended the church I first pastored. As a teenager, she lost her father. This trauma led to patterns of thinking that led to an abusive relationship, resulting in a child out of wedlock. After the child's birth, this young lady turned to Christ. For several years, she did well serving the Lord. She even graduated from Bible school. During this time, her mother was murdered. This additional trauma eventually caused her old patterns of thinking to resurface. This led to an abusive marriage in which she had another child. However, it ended in divorce. Broken and suffering, she returned to the church. After this, she ended up in yet another marriage filled with abuse. Another child came from that marriage. She divorced that man and was left with three children to take care of on her own. Yet, she came back to church. Today, she is serving the Lord with her three lovely children.

Watching her go through this was difficult for me. On more than one occasion, I wanted to give up on her and leave her to her choices. But not the Lord. She is His. This woman's many testimonies show how the Lord extended His mercy and grace and got her through her trials. God was front and present. I can say the same thing about my own failures. When I am ready to give up on myself, God's presence isn't far.

Have you had repeated failures—maybe even a lifetime of failures—that have caused you untold suffering? Like the disciples, can you attest to God's faithfulness despite them?

That is a wink from God. You are still *His* disciple. His presence, demonstrated by His faithfulness, is proof that He is at work in our own failures. We can hope—and we can trust—that He is making things right. Our success as disciples has more to do with His faithfulness to us than our faithfulness to Him.

Wink #17

GOD WINKS IN ANTICIPATION OF OUR FAILURES

Our failures don't surprise God. We can take solace in this. He saw them coming; He knew they would happen. But more than anticipating our failures and the suffering they bring, the Lord has provided for our restoration and redemption. Where is God when we fail? He's writing more to our story through His mercy and grace.

Our failures are but a chapter in the grand story of our redemption. Can God redeem something from the suffering we've caused ourselves? The Scriptures wink to let us know He can. In Matthew's Gospel this comes to us in another intercalation that takes place between Matthew 26:30–75.

The first part (verses 30–35) takes place on the night Jesus is betrayed and arrested before His crucifixion. Jesus and His disciples are on the Mount of Olives. Jesus tells them they all would abandon Him that very evening. Peter insists that it is not so and vows never to leave Jesus's side. Anticipating Peter's failure to come, Jesus prophesies, *"This very night, before the rooster crows, you will deny me **three times"*** (verse 34).

Following this, Jesus is betrayed and arrested by the chief priests and elders. At the home of Caiaphas, the high priest, Jesus is questioned and ridiculed. The religious leaders spit in Jesus's face, strike Him with their fists, and taunt Him, saying, *"Prophesy to us, you Christ! Who is it that struck you?"* (verse 68). In their estimation, if He was the Christ, He could prophesy to them. If He had prophesied correctly, perhaps *some* might have rethought what they were doing. But Jesus remains silent.

I used to read this part of the story and think, *Jesus, why didn't You just say something?* One side of me wishes He would have told them things about their lives. This is where the irony of Scripture is brilliant. This is where the wink comes in.

In the next part (verses 69–75), Peter is found in the courtyard. In three instances, people recognize him as one of Jesus's disciples and in each case, Peter denies it. The words of Christ—His prophesy in the first section (verses 30–35)—has come to pass.

These three sections form an intercalation that looks like this:

+ Part I: Jesus tells Peter he will deny Him three times (Matthew 26:30–35)

  » Intercalation: Jesus is mocked and told to prophesy, but He doesn't (verses 57–68)

+ Part II: Jesus's prophesy about Peter is fulfilled (verses 69–75)

The middle section comments on the two sections that frame it. Here lies the wink and the irony. At the same time that religious leaders are mocking Jesus because He won't prophesy, Peter is in the courtyard denying Jesus, just as Christ prophesied. Jesus didn't have to prophesy to the religious leaders. His prophecy was being fulfilled right outside in the courtyard where they aren't looking.

JESUS DIDN'T HAVE TO PROPHESY TO THE
RELIGIOUS LEADERS. HIS PROPHECY WAS BEING
FULFILLED RIGHT OUTSIDE IN THE COURTYARD
WHERE THEY AREN'T LOOKING.

The way Matthew sets up this story is a wink that suggests that Jesus is Lord and Messiah. He's signaling to us that Jesus is the Christ while the high priest is saying He is not. The Lord is standing before them, and they don't realize it.

As Messiah, Jesus predicted and anticipated Peter's shortcomings and prophesied these to him. But the Messiah doesn't stop with that. There is more work to be done besides anticipating failure. The Messiah is later found on the cross. He suffers for Peter's failure. Jesus goes to the cross precisely for the brokenness in Peter that caused him to abandon his Lord. He is not allowing Peter's failure to be the end of Him. In the midst of Peter's suffering, God is found writing a longer chapter for the apostle—a chapter of restoration and redemption, through his own suffering.

Perhaps you have recently failed and now you are suffering because of it. Do you think your failure has put God's grace at risk in your life? Don't bet on it. God has never been surprised by anything you've done. If anyone is to be surprised, it's you.

This is also the case for the rest of the world. Humanity fails. Governments fail. Policy fails. This failure results in suffering of untold proportions. I don't want to oversimply the complexity of events that cause suffering or undermine the unexplainable sorrow and grief they bring. But it is nevertheless true that God expected this failure from the beginning.

Anticipating this failure, He went to the cross and suffered as Lord and Messiah so He could restore mankind from all of their mistakes and sins that have brought such sorrow. In His suffering, He has written a longer chapter. Along with its cruelty and sorrow, the history of the world is given God's grand scheme, a small story that makes up the bigger story of God's great grace and restoration through Christ Jesus the Lord.

The next time you fail, have a friend who fails, or see failure in the world, remind yourself that Jesus is the Messiah. He has anticipated this failure. He said it would happen. And He winks. He has met that failure by His work on the cross.

So, the story doesn't end with failure or the suffering it causes. There is more to it than that. There is a much bigger story that involves our restoration and redemption. All because the Lord, who anticipated we would suffer for our failures, has suffered on our behalf.

Wink #18

GOD WINKS IN OUR PACING

Have you ever spent a sleepless night burning a hole in the carpet, pacing the floor? I'm a pacer. When I'm suffering within, I move about aimlessly, wondering what to do.

Not too long ago, I moved out of the townhouse that had been my home for ten years. While packing, I found a photo that was taken when I first moved in. Right then, I snapped a picture of the same spot from the same angle. I compared the two photos, side by side. Two photos separated by a decade of time. The first thing I noticed was the worn-out carpet. Its plushness was decimated and gone. I imagine a lot of that wear and tear was the result of my pacing back and forth, suffering something internally that kept me from a good night's rest.

But those times of internal suffering weren't a total waste of time. In them, the Lord drew me to act and do what I *knew* He was leading me to do. In my pacing, He was subtly winking, bidding me in my internal suffering to obey. But don't just take my word for it. Examine your own life. Has the Lord tried to evoke your obedience when you were having your own inward crisis?

Where is God when you are suffering something internally? As you pace the floor, He's speaking to you in a still, small voice. (See 1 Kings 19:12.)

In the Gospel of John, we are presented with a pacer—someone walking back and forth with such unease that it becomes uncomfortable to watch. The man is suffering something profound within. It even seems he's going somewhat mad.

Is the Lord present in this? To tease out the wink, we must know how John adds this man to the story. John does this by manipulating the setting.

The setting is the background in which the story takes place. It can be a physical or a social location. By paying attention to the setting, the audience can glean more than what is simply stated by the author. The setting often implies subtle nuances that the author wants readers to discover for themselves. These serve as winks.

Before looking at the settings in the biblical narrative, let's examine the setting in a popular movie that many of us have seen, Alfred Hitchcock's 1960 thriller, *Psycho*.

Psycho is about a woman named Marion Crane who steals $40,000 from her boss. She leaves town with it, heading from Phoenix, Arizona, to her boyfriend's home in Fairvale, California. En route, she stops at the Bates Motel to spend the night. Bad idea.

The owner, Norman Bates, invites her to dinner when she checks in. Unbeknownst to her, Norman is a psychopath with two personalities. After their dinner, Marion has a change of heart and decides she will return to Phoenix the next day and give back the money she stole. She prepares for bed and takes a shower. This is the moment of her doom. Slowly, Norman Bates—masked and disguised—enters the bathroom and murders the unsuspecting damsel.

The setting in *Psycho* complements the inner turmoil we observe in Marion's behavior. There are two cities involved: Phoenix and Fairvale. The setting is divided, just as Marion is about her decisions. We observe Marion's internal struggle as we follow her along the way. She drives from Phoenix toward Fairvale and later decides to return to Phoenix.

Her hesitant travel between the towns reveals her own internal conflict of desires. On one hand, she desires to steal the money and run away with her boyfriend. On the other, she desires to be honest and right her wrongs. Her back-and-forth indicates she is suffering internally, conflicted, and wrestling in her soul.

This setting is perfect for *Psycho*. Perhaps it's not just the Norman Bateses of the world who wrestle in their souls, divided between desires. Aren't we all crazy in our own way? This might make the audience realize they have their own issues within, although they aren't psychotic. Perhaps it will prompt them to deal with their problems and act with integrity so they don't end up like Marion. This is how powerful manipulating the setting can be.

In John's gospel, the apostle manipulates the setting for effect. It reveals a lot about what's going on inside the character he's presenting—Pontius Pilate, the Roman governor of Judea. In return, we examine ourselves.

IN THE GOSPEL OF JOHN, THE SETTING WORKS TO SHOW US THAT PILATE IS SUFFERING INNER TURMOIL ABOUT WHETHER THE INNOCENT JESUS WILL BE CRUCIFIED.

We find Pilate in John 18:28–19:16. Jesus is brought to the Roman praetorium before His crucifixion. By this point in the story, it is up to Pilate to decide whether the innocent Jesus will be crucified. The setting works to show us that Pilate is suffering inner turmoil about making this decision. How do we know?

He's pacing back and forth. Like Marion Crane's planned back-and-forth drive between Fairvale and Phoenix, Pilate is divided between Jesus inside the praetorium and the crowd on the outside. Notice:

> **So Pilate went outside to them** and said, "What accusation do you bring against this man?" (John 18:29)

> **So Pilate entered his headquarters again** and called Jesus and said to him, "Are you the King of the Jews?" (John 18:33)

> After he had said this, **he went back outside to the Jews** and told them, "I find no guilt in him." (John 18:38)

> Then Pilate took Jesus and flogged him...**Pilate went out again and said to them**, "See, I am bringing him out to you that you may know that I find no guilt in him." (John 19:1, 4)

> **He entered his headquarters again** and said to Jesus, "Where are you from?" But Jesus gave him no answer. (John 19:9)

> So, when Pilate heard these words, **he brought Jesus out** and sat down on the judgment seat at a place called The Stone Pavement, and in Aramaic Gabbatha. (John 19:13)

Pilate, suffering because he's unsure what to do, swings back and forth between what Jesus says and what the crowd says. He's troubled. Conflicted. Wrestling. The more pressure he gets from the crowd, the more intense the uneasiness in his soul becomes. This attests not only to the innocence of Jesus but also to the vindictiveness of the crowd.

The setting's hidden subtlety is a wink. It challenges us to explore our hearts. When we are divided and suffer because of our own inner turmoil, will we choose Christ? Or will we go with the crowd?

> ## WHEN WE ARE DIVIDED AND SUFFER BECAUSE OF OUR OWN INNER TURMOIL, WILL WE CHOOSE CHRIST? OR WILL WE GO WITH THE CROWD?

The crowd represents the voice that directs us to make the wrong decision. This includes our own voice. As long as we welcome the crowd, we'll keep burning holes in the carpet with uneasy pacing. We'll keep going in and out of the praetorium. The longer we refuse to obey, the more needless suffering we will experience, and the deeper our turmoil will grow.

Eusebius records Pilate eventually committed suicide during the reign of Caligula in AD 37 to 41. He wrote:

> It is worthy of note that Pilate himself, who was governor in the time of our Saviour, is reported to have fallen into such misfortunes under Caius, whose times we are recording, that he was forced to become his own murderer and executioner; and thus, divine vengeance, as it seems, was not long in overtaking him.[9]

If you've been pacing lately, you're at a fork in the road. God is winking in this. He's in the center of your uneasiness, amid your turmoil, bidding you to obey Him. See your pacing as an opportunity to do what's right, to return to integrity. Will your pacing

---

9. See Eusebius of Caesaria, "The Church History of Eusebius," in *Eusebius: Church History, Life of Constantine the Great, and Oration in Praise of Constantine*, ed. Philip Schaff and Henry Wace, trans. Arthur Cushman McGiffert, vol. 1, *A Select Library of the Nicene and Post-Nicene Fathers of the Christian Church*, Second Series (New York, NY: Christian Literature Company, 1890), 110.

lead to further uneasiness or will it lead to rest in your soul? Don't be divided any longer. Choose to side with Christ. Can you sense Him in your pacing? What's He telling you to do?

Wink #19

GOD WINKS IN OUR INNER TURMOIL

Inner turmoil is a profound form of human suffering. Whether it's looking back with regret on the mistakes we've made, or dealing with rejection, an existential crisis, or anything in between, the human race suffers from pain in the soul. Sadly, this pain often drives humans in the wrong direction. Severe cases of pain may lead to substance abuse, depression, loss of hope, a lack of motivation, damage to relationships, and even self-harm or suicide. It might feel impossible to discern where God is when our souls are shaded in the darkness.

Bleak as that may be, God winks in our inner turmoil. I'd like to share a story that invites this hope. While I realize it is not as severe as a major depressive disorder or the chaos caused by spousal betrayal, it does illustrate God's nearness to our humanness and pain. That can encourage those of us affected by more severe forms of emotional trauma.

I was talking to a colleague—another professor of theology—about the nearness of God and how He often surprises us in ways that disrupt our closely held dogmas. Relevant to this conversation is the fact that my colleague grew up in church that taught cessationism. This is the theological belief that spiritual gifts ceased with the close of Apostolic Age.

Though he remained suspicious about cessationism, it caused him to have low expectations that God would move in supernatural ways within his life. Sure, he believed God is sovereign and could orchestrate divine events and perform miracles. But to see this in his own life? He didn't wake up each day thinking that a miracle could happen to *him*.

Before our conversation, his cousin had passed away. Since he and his cousin were only a few months apart in age, this caused my colleague to have an existential crisis. He was approaching age sixty and pondered his own existence, purpose, and the effect his life had had up to that point. Though he was a wonderful husband and father, a brilliant communicator, a successful pastor, and beloved professor, he still wondered if his life even mattered. His ponderings led toward sadness and despair.

He and his wife drove to the funeral in Chicago. On the way back to their home in Detroit, he had a desire to stop at a Cracker Barrel restaurant for dinner.

"I never eat there, Chris. Ever. I don't even know why I wanted to go so badly."

He approached the hostess stand and asked for a table. The hostess, a burly, middle-aged woman, thundered a deep belly laugh, "Boy, I tell ya! I'm so glad I get to wait on you today! You look like a pastor to me, sir. Are you a pastor?"

Shocked, he stammered, "Why, why yes, yes. I am. I am a pastor."

"Good!" she exclaimed. "I am going to give you a great seat today!"

While telling this story, my colleague was laughing hysterically. "Chris, this woman had never seen me in her life. She had no idea who I was. And I have no idea how she knew I was a pastor. It was the oddest moment I've ever experienced."

As he continued to tell me the story, it grew increasingly bizarre. After they finished dining, his wife wanted to shop in the little country store that all Cracker Barrels have. While browsing, the ebullient hostess approached him.

"Sir, I'd like to sing a song to you."

He looked at her with disbelief, one eyebrow arched, "Um, o-o-k. I guess that would be f-i-n-e."

The rotund hostess boomed out a hymn so loud the whole shop overheard it. She was singing the blessings of God over his life.

"Chris," my colleague exclaimed, "you won't believe what she said when she finished singing. You just won't believe it!"

I had a good idea what was coming next.

She said, "Sir, I just want you to know that God says your life matters. Your. Life. Matters!"

Now, explain that.

My colleague and friend knows that the God of the universe is paying attention to little old him. God is concerned about his emotional well-being and his inner turmoil. And God subtly winked in this professor's suffering in a most unusual way—through a jolly old Cracker Barrel hostess.

GOD WINKS IN UNUSUAL WAYS WHEN WE FIND OURSELVES IN THE SHADOW OF DISTRESS.

If you are in a state of emotional suffering, there's reason to hope. God winks in unusual ways when we find ourselves in the shadow of distress. This is Peter's case in John 21.

Here we discover Peter experiencing inner turmoil for having denied Christ. John makes use of props in this story to show readers how God winks at the suffering apostle and initiates his healing and restoration.

Props are objects that show up in a story. Like the setting, they, too, can be a wink. For example, let's go back to the movie *Psycho*. The most well-known prop in this movie is the knife that Norman Bates uses to kill Marion in the shower. Have you ever wondered why he uses a knife? Norman had killed many women before Marion. Since this was his modus operandi, why didn't he invest in a gun? What could the knife represent?

At the end of the movie, a psychiatrist reveals that Norman often believed he was his own mother, whom he had also killed. Whenever Norman became interested in a woman, "mother" would get jealous, and Norman (as "mother") would kill the woman. The murders are tied to jealousy.

The knife, piercing the woman, represents Norman's perverted sense of sexuality. It adds to the twistedness of his mind and heightens the horror of the movie. The audience might come away with a renewed revulsion for sexual perversion. Perhaps they may even wonder what boundaries they should set about sexuality. All this, from a simple prop.

The New Testament uses props for powerful effect. We often overlook them and fail to consider the subtleties to which they may allude. By considering the props, we find outstanding discoveries, little winks that are exciting.

In John 21:1–14, the Lord appears to the disciples after they desert Him. This time they are out fishing on the water, about a hundred yards from land. Jesus is standing on the shore, but the disciples don't realize it's the Lord. He asks the disciples for fish, but they hadn't caught any. In true Jesus fashion, He tells the disciples to cast their net to the right side of the boat. They do so and get a huge catch. They realize it could only be the Lord, and they rush to shore.

Peter is especially excited. Jesus makes breakfast for them and reinstates Peter, who had recently denied Him. (See John 21:15–19.) Great story, right? There's something even better about it we shouldn't overlook. It takes us into the psychology of Peter's state of mind.

John indicates that Jesus has prepared breakfast on a *"charcoal fire"* (verse 9). We might be tempted to read right over this, but this prop is a wink. It has real significance.

This isn't the first time we see a charcoal fire appear as a prop in John's gospel. It also crops up on the night Peter denied Jesus.

> Now the servants and officers had made a **charcoal fire**, because it was cold, and they were standing and warming themselves. Peter also was with them, standing and warming himself. (John 18:18)

Peter was warming himself by the *"charcoal fire"* as he was in the process of denying Christ.

Have you ever smelled a charcoal fire? Strong, isn't it? The smell of burning charcoal is one of my favorite summertime smells. No matter where I smell it now, it immediately jogs my memory and takes me right back to Kensington Metro Park in Milford, Michigan, where I would often barbeque hamburgers with my friends on summer evenings. For me, the smell of charcoal evokes comfort, peace, and a sense that everything is all right in the world.

I doubt Peter had the same sentiments about charcoal. It's not much of a stretch to consider that the smell of charcoal would have thrown Peter into inner turmoil. It would have jogged Peter's memory, taking him back to the night when he denied the One he so loved.

The charcoal fire would have produced suffering. It was more than just charcoal. The smell drew Peter's attention back to his own spineless actions that Jesus was about to confront. Did Jesus use the charcoal to draw that inner turmoil out of Peter so He could confront it and restore him? Yep. The charcoal is another subtle wink. Jesus knew Peter's pain, was familiar with his suffering, and wasn't going to let him stay that way.

God knows our inner turmoil. He knows when we are having a crisis within. Though it may feel like we are battling this suffering alone, God is at work in it, and He is with us.

Whether it be a Cracker Barrel hostess or a charcoal fire, God has unusual ways of winking when our souls are shaded in darkness. These subtle winks give us the hope we need to heal. Don't give up. God has a plan to heal and restore you. Expect Him to wink in your turmoil, bleak as it may seem.

Wink #20

GOD WINKS IN LANTERNS
AND TORCHES

King David committed a terrible sin. He used his power to commit adultery with Bathsheba, another man's wife. When she told him that she was pregnant, David tried to get her husband, Uriah, one of his elite soldiers, to sleep with her to cover up his crime. Uriah refused to do this because his men were still off fighting. So David put Uriah on the front lines of battle to be killed. (See 2 Samuel 11.) This was cold-blooded, premeditated murder combined with the abuse of his authority as king. Bad idea.

Earlier, I defined suffering as the experience of any pain, whether emotional, physical, mental, relational, or spiritual. Examples include those who lose everything because of natural disasters or those harmed in sudden accidents. That suffering is out of our control.

Yet, there is a suffering we do control. It comes because of our own disobedience. When disobedience catches up with us—and it will—the consequences can produce angst, distress, and profound turmoil in our soul. We see an example of such suffering in Psalm 51, a well-known psalm of David.

WHEN DISOBEDIENCE CATCHES UP WITH US, THE CONSEQUENCES CAN PRODUCE ANGST, DISTRESS, AND PROFOUND TURMOIL IN OUR SOUL.

King David's depravity caught up with him when he was confronted by the prophet Nathan. (See 2 Samuel 12:1–12.) David was mortified.

> *David said to Nathan, "I have sinned against the LORD." And Nathan said to David, "The LORD also has put away your sin; you shall not die. Nevertheless, because by this deed you have utterly scorned the LORD, the child who is born to you shall die."* (2 Samuel 12:13–14)

Scholars believe that David's sorrowful Psalm 51 comes between the moment David admits that he has sinned and the time that passes while he awaits the consequences of his disobedience. (See 2 Samuel 12:13–14.) God does show the king mercy. However, despite God's mercy, the son of his union with Bathsheba dies. David grieves the child's death with bitterness and heartache. (See verses 16–23.)

Much can be drawn from this story about Israel's history, the character of God, and Israel's need for a righteous king, Jesus. It also paints an ominous portrait of sin, detailed in Psalm 51 with brushstrokes of suffering. Readers are left with the impression that our own depravity is cause for our suffering. The psalmist begs God to save him from both. As Christian readers, we are left with stark contrast: we can choose disobedience and suffering, or we can choose righteousness and peace. The story of David confronts us with this choice.

Can you think of a time when you chose the former? What were the consequences? I have made my own fair share of bad choices and suffered the consequences. I've wasted money, lost friendships, and hurt people created in the image of God. And, of course, feeling like a slimeball adds insult to injury. Disobedience is walking in the darkness. There's suffering in that darkness.

This is illustrated in the story of Judas. The way John narrates his disobedience winks at us. In this wink, we find God (as always) prompting us to choose obedience so we can avoid sorrow and suffering.

To appreciate how John portrays Judas, we need to understand a bit about irony, which is a literary technique that distorts the obvious meaning of something so that it means something more. Its added meaning is unexpected and surprising. I tell my students they have spotted irony when something makes them say, "Aha!"

John is a master of irony. To appreciate the irony he sets around Judas, we need to know that John has already used themes of darkness and light throughout his gospel. (See, for example, John 1:4–5; 8:12; 9:5.) In John 11:9–10, Jesus says, "*If anyone walks in the day, he does not stumble, because he sees **the light of this world**. But if anyone **walks in the night**, he stumbles, because **the light is not in him**.*"

JESUS USES THE METAPHOR OF LIGHT TO DESCRIBE HIMSELF. HE USES DARKNESS TO REFER TO SIN AND SEPARATION FROM GOD.

Jesus uses the metaphor of light to describe Himself. He uses darkness to refer to sin and separation from God, which in Judas's case, will result from an exceedingly poor choice he makes. This sets the stage for what happens when Judas leaves the Passover Seder at *night* to betray Jesus.

> *So, after receiving the morsel of bread, [Judas] immediately went out. And it was **night**.*   (John 13:30)

This is ironic. John isn't *just* referring to the time of day. He means more. Because John has used "night" to refer to sin, John suggests that Judas's choice to betray Jesus is sinful. He goes out into the darkness of his own pitiable choice. When we choose disobedience, we go off into similar darkness. And, as we saw in David's case, there is suffering in that darkness.

John develops the irony while Jesus is in the garden of Gethsemane. In chapter 18, Jesus and His disciples leave the Passover Seder and head toward the garden. It's worth noting that He and His disciples get to the garden from the room where they've had Passover with no trouble. (See verse 1.) It's an uneventful walk. John does not explain that.

Yet, John adds an ironic detail when he talks about how Judas gets to the garden. More props show up—this time, lanterns and torches.

*So Judas, having procured a band of soldiers and some officers from the chief priests and the Pharisees, **went there with lanterns and torches** and weapons.* (John 18:3)

Why does John mention that Judas needed lanterns and torches but doesn't say that Jesus and His company needed them? John is winking at us by telling us this. Aha! Scripture is emphasizing that Judas was walking in the darkness. Without Jesus, he had no light. It goes back to what John records in 11:9–10: those who walk at night will stumble because they have no light. Judas's choice to betray Jesus leads to darkness, even separation from God. The eventual consequences of this darkness are tragic suffering and pain. (See Matthew 27:1–10.)

This whole account winks at us. It highlights the catastrophic nature of disobedience and living separated from God. It also shows us that humans can be the cause of their own suffering. When we choose disobedience, we choose to be vexed and disquieted by the consequences of that sin. David lost his child. Judas committed suicide.

THE ACCOUNT OF JUDAS AND THE SOLDIERS NEEDING LANTERNS AND TORCHES TO GET TO JESUS IN THE GARDEN HIGHLIGHTS THE CATASTROPHIC NATURE OF DISOBEDIENCE AND LIVING SEPARATED FROM GOD.

While our disobedience doesn't always lead to such drastic results, is even the smallest pang in our soul worth it? Personally, I have never been glad when I've disobeyed God. Instead, I've found myself in the darkness, unsettled and unhinged. And like King David, I cry out to God for mercy. Each instance could have been avoided had I simply chosen to walk in the light and not plunge into the night.

The next time you face a choice to walk in light or stumble around at night, remember David. Remember Judas and company. Remember the lanterns and the torches. They subtly wink.

Christ is the true Light. Without Him, we will err in darkness and suffer because of it. Don't cause your own demise. God is present when we are faced with a choice where disobedience will lead to our own suffering. Being present, He bids us to walk in the light—not to go into the night without Him.

Wink #21

GOD WINKS IN THE MARGINALIZED

What can be said about those whose suffering is not caused by their own decisions? What about those at the margins—the ones who suffer because they have been sidelined against their will due to socioeconomic status and the situation into which they were born? Where is God in their suffering? The ministry of Jesus speaks *a lot* to this.

The gospel writers consistently portray Christ at work in the suffering of the marginalized, reinstating the banished and embracing those whom society has overlooked. This includes lepers, the poor, the blind, the lame, vilified ethnicities, and even women of ill repute. Scripture never explains why one is born into plush circumstances and another into want. What Scripture does tell us, however, is that God is at work in the margins. Through Christ, God is doing something extraordinary. His work and ministry in the Gospels reveal this.

Pope Francis acknowledges this. In one of his homilies, he says, "For Jesus, what matters above all is reaching out to save those far off, healing the wounds of the sick, restoring everyone to God's family...He wanted to reinstate the outcast, to save those outside the camp." Pope Francis refers to God's treatment of the marginalized as the "logic" of Jesus.

According to Pope Francis, *the church* is now responsible to represent Christ to these people in their sorrow. He urges his cardinals to share in Christ's ministry and "to serve Jesus crucified in every person who is emarginated, for whatever reason; to see the Lord in every excluded person...We will not find the Lord unless we truly accept the marginalized!"[10]

God now works among the marginalized through those who will serve them. The whole narrative in Matthew speaks to this. If we examine the text as a whole, we find a subtle wink that confirms it and prompts His body to be the relief of innocent sufferers though the gospel.

To understand this, we need to examine Matthew 1:1–17, which gives us the genealogy of Jesus. Readers often skip this chapter, not sure why a bunch of unpronounceable names should matter. However, we shouldn't shortchange this section. There's a lot to be discovered. For one thing, it includes five women in Jesus's lineage, four of whom are gentiles. This is especially surprising because, in those times, lineages didn't usually include a woman's name. Even more surprising, these four gentile women aren't the kind of people you might expect to find among the Messiah's ancestors.

First, there is Tamar. (See Matthew 1:3.) Tamar posed as a prostitute and solicited her father-in-law, Judah, for sex without him knowing. (See Genesis 38.) She did this because both of her previous husbands had died, and she was without a child. She was suffering. Marginalized. Without a child, she did not have a future

---

10. Pope Francis, "Holy Mass with the New Cardinals: Homily of His Holiness Pope Francis," Vatican Basilica, February 15, 2015, www.vatican.va/content/francesco/en/homilies/2015/documents/papa-francesco_20150215_omelia-nuovi-cardinali.html.

or any social security. By having sex with Judah and getting pregnant with his child, she was attempting to protect herself.

Next, we find Rahab, a prostitute from Jericho. (See Joshua 2.) She had heard the miraculous stories that God had done on behalf of the Israelites. She feared and revered the Lord. Clearly, she wanted out of her lifestyle as a scorned prostitute. She hid the Israelite spies before the Israelites defeated Jericho and went on to marry a Jew. Together, they had Boaz, who eventually marries Ruth.

Ruth is the third gentile woman in Christ's lineage. Ruth was a follower of Yahweh, though she was a Moabite. (See Ruth 3.) However, she was without a husband and without a provider. Marginalized. Yet, Boaz marries her, and they have a son together, Obed, who would become the grandfather of King David.

The fourth marginalized gentile woman in Jesus's lineage is called *"the wife of Uriah"* (verse 6). This was, of course, Bathsheba. After Uriah is killed in battle, David marries her but the child of their adulterous relationship dies. Eventually, she gives birth to Solomon, who becomes David's successor to the throne.

THE LOGIC OF JESUS IS DIFFERENT.
GOD, IN CHRIST, SEEKS THE MARGINALIZED AND
MAKES A PLACE FOR THEM IN HIS KINGDOM,
DESPITE THEIR SOCIAL SITUATION AND THE
SUFFERING CAUSED BY IT.

It is interesting that four women who suffered marginalization find themselves in the lineage of Jesus. God does not exclude them. They aren't excluded because of wrongdoing, they aren't excluded because they are gentiles, and they aren't excluded because of their gender. God has made a place for them. He sees fit to include those who, by the religious and social standards of the day, were wronged for all the "right" reasons. But the logic of Jesus is different. God, in Christ, seeks the marginalized and makes a place for them in His kingdom, despite their social situation and the suffering caused by it.

After examining the first chapter of Matthew and noting the women in Christ's lineage, we jump to the end of Matthew's gospel, chapter 28, and find another subtle wink. Jesus tells His disciples, *"Go therefore and make disciples of all nations"* (verse 19). The term *"nations"* suggests the gospel is not just for Jews. The family of God is extended to the gentile people of the earth. Many of those gentiles were those at the margins—people suffering because of social and economic status over which they had no control, like the four gentile women in Christ's lineage.

These four women and Jesus's command to make disciples of all nations form an inclusio around the entirety of Matthew. It looks like this:

+ Gentile women in Christ's lineage (Matthew 1:1–25)

   » Matthew's gospel (Matthew 2–28)

+ Jesus's command to make disciples of the gentiles (Matthew 28:19–20)

THE MINISTRY OF JESUS IS ABOUT EXTENDING THE GOOD NEWS OF GRACE TO ALL THE NATIONS OF THE EARTH, INCLUDING THOSE AT THE MARGINS.

This inclusio is a wink that shows the ministry of Jesus, in Matthew's gospel, is about extending the good news of grace to *all* the nations of the earth, including those at the margins. Jesus didn't limit His kingdom to the pious Jews. He came for the whole world *and* for those whom the whole world least expected—those who suffer as the weak and the lowly. His love extends to every woman who is a victim of sex trafficking, to all prostitutes who have sold their bodies to make a living, to every individual who has been trampled upon by the power structures of the world, and to those born in nations where hunger and starvation abound.

Where is God in the suffering of those at the margins? How does He work in their despair? Scripture tells us that He works though His body, the church, which He has called to preach the gospel and serve the suffering.

Pope Francis insists:

> The compassion of Jesus! That *com-passion* which made him [Jesus] draw near to every person in pain! Jesus does not hold back; instead, he gets involved in people's pain and their need.[11]

When you look into the darkness and ponder the innocent suffering that goes on all over the world among the marginalized, remember the four gentile women. Remember the call to preach the gospel.

Now, the Lord invites *you* to call the marginalized. Tell them what God has done about sin and evil through Jesus. Invite them to follow, to be part of God's family. Show them goodness and charity. Bring relief to the suffering they didn't choose for themselves. It may even be that when you show up, they will have been wondering about their own suffering, uncertain what to make of it.

Through you, they will see God wink in their darkness. You'll give them hope beyond a world where people are born into sorrow.

---

11. Ibid.

Wink #22

GOD WINKS AT HIS BANQUET TABLE

Our fallen world cannot produce a perfect system in which there is no injustice. No matter what economic system or political structure a nation or society has, there will always be a sidelined group of poor people. Jesus tells us this. (See Matthew 26:11.) The result is suffering. For as long as we live, we suffer. For as long as we are under broken human systems, we will be broken.

But there is hope. Scripture gives us a subtle wink.

God tells us that His coming kingdom is the ultimate answer to those suffering under the system. Luke's gospel alludes to this, showing us in a rather interesting way that God is near the sidelined.

Through Luke's text, we notice that a lot takes place around the table. Rich theology is posited in times of banqueting. Have you ever noticed that Luke records ten different meals in his gospel? On ten occasions, we see events taking place while people eat. This shouldn't be overlooked.

Here is a list of these meals:

Banquet Scene	Verses in Luke	Key Person(s)
Levi's home	5:27–32	Tax collectors and sinners
Pharisee's home	7:36–50	Uninvited sinful woman
Near Bethsaida	9:10–17	The multitudes
Mary and Martha's home	10:38–42	Mary and Martha
Pharisee's home	11:37–54	Scribes and Pharisees
Home of important Pharisee	14:1–24	Man suffering from swelling
Zacchaeus's home	19:1–10	Zacchaeus, a lost sinner
Passover meal in Jerusalem	22:7–38	Disciples
Near the village of Emmaus	24:13–35	Cleopas and another person
Jerusalem	24:36–53	Disciples

It's important to note that Jesus presides over all of these scenes. The intimate table fellowship is centered on Him. This points to meals being more than just mundane settings in Luke. They theologize. What they represent is the coming eschatological kingdom of God. It signals that one day, Jesus will be all in all. His creation will dine with Him in His kingdom. The meal scenes further represent whom He has invited to sit with Him at His table.

JESUS PRESIDES OVER ALL OF THE BANQUET
SCENES IN LUKE. THEY REPRESENT THE
COMING ESCHATOLOGICAL KINGDOM OF GOD,
WHEN WE WILL DINE WITH HIM.

And like most stories in the Gospels, there is plenty of irony and unexpected outcomes that make us wonder. They cause us to think about what God is doing amidst the broken systems in our world to ultimately solve the problem of suffering.

The first irony in Luke's story is that those who would be most expected to have a seat at the table, the religious leaders and Pharisees, are rebuked while they sit with Jesus. This happens in the fifth meal scene. (See Luke 11:37–54.) Jesus's rebuke is so harsh that one scribe comments, *"Teacher, in saying these things you insult us also"* (verse 45).

However, Jesus doesn't stop. He continues to prod them. (See Luke 11:46–52). Jesus's criticism suggests that the Pharisees were hypocrites. They didn't make ideal guests at His table. This becomes more shocking when Jesus tells us who *is* invited to His table:

> *When you give a dinner or a banquet, do not invite your friends or your brothers or your relatives or rich neighbors, lest they also invite you in return and you be repaid. But when you give a feast, invite the poor, the crippled, the lame, the blind, and you will be blessed, because they cannot repay you.*
> (Luke 14:12–14; compare Luke 14:15–24)

Jesus invited the marginalized to His table—those who had been chewed up and spit out by the system. They were the "losers" who were used up by the world's broken societal schemes. This sidelined bunch of sufferers are the ones who will dine with Jesus at His table in His kingdom. Not the manipulators but the manipulated.

Irony like this is found in every meal scene. In the first scene (5:27–32), Jesus shares a meal in the home of a tax collector named Levi, who *"made [Jesus] a great feast in his house, and there was a large company of tax collectors and others reclining at table with them"* (verse 29). These people were sinners who didn't live up to the religious standards of the day. In fact, they took advantage of the poor. They *were* the system. Yet Jesus is interested in them. He invites them to repent. He wants them to be part of His kingdom.

Since this is the first instance that Jesus has a meal in Luke, it sets the tone for what to expect when Jesus presides over a banquet. The reader gets a sense that Jesus will approach all the "wrong" people. Not only is Jesus inviting the manipulated, but He's also inviting the manipulators. What is going on? By inviting the system to *His* system, Jesus was demonstrating that He can restore all things.

BY INVITING BOTH THE MANIPULATED AND THE MANIPULATORS TO THESE BANQUETS, JESUS IS DEMONSTRATING THAT HE CAN RESTORE ALL THINGS.

In the second meal scene (7:36–50), Jesus is at a banquet in the home of a Pharisee. A sinful woman shows up. The ironic part is that she had not been invited by the host. Yet, Jesus welcomes her. He refuses to condemn her for her sin. Instead, He accepts the woman's gift. He forgives her sins. He tells her to go in peace. Jesus welcomes the unwelcomed to His table.

In the third scene (9:10–17), there's more irony. Jesus feeds the crowd near Bethsaida. The crowd includes the dejected, the hungry, and the lost. Jesus, as the host, doesn't just give them a snack to partially satisfy them. He gives them so much to eat that there were twelve baskets left over. (See verse 17.) This shows that Jesus has every intention of satisfying those whom He invites into His kingdom. Unlike the broken systems we suffer under, in Christ's kingdom, there is enough to go around with plenty left over. Every sufferer is fulfilled in Christ.

In the fourth scene (10:38–42), Jesus comes to the home of Mary and Martha to dine. This is ironic. In Christ's day, it was virtually unheard of for women to be disciples. Yet Mary is learning from Jesus, and Jesus urges Martha to do the same. (See verses 41–42.) This shows that the guest list for Jesus's kingdom is subversive and unconventional. It's not just a good ol' boys' club. The least likely are on Jesus's guest list.

In the fifth banquet scene in Luke 14:1–24, Jesus is dining at another Pharisee's home. A man who's suffering from excess fluid retention (dropsy) shows up. In ancient times, his condition was associated with sexual sin and demon possession. Whether this was true in his case is beside the point. He was a social outcast, looked down on for his sickness. Definitely not the kind of person a Pharisee invites to his home. Yet, Jesus welcomes him to the banquet. He embraces this sufferer as a guest. Then, He heals him. Again, we are shown that social outcasts and losers in the systems are invited to sup in Christ's eschatological kingdom. The healing represents Christ's ability to make all things well, physically, socially, and even economically. He will end all suffering in His kingdom.

In the seventh banquet scene, Jesus encounters the rich tax collector named Zacchaeus. (See Luke 19:1–10.) Zacchaeus is short, so he had to climb a tree to find Jesus, but Jesus finds him. (See verses 4–5.)

Plot twist here: Jesus is back to hanging out with the manipulators. What's the deal? Jesus isn't against extending His kingdom to those who have caused the suffering of the broken. He is at work in this world, doing something about the evil that has caused so much sorrow. If He can restore those who are broken, He can restore those who have done the breaking.

This story illustrates *we should write no one off*. Jesus invites Himself to stay at Zacchaeus's house and presides over the banquet with this thief and criminal, who repents and agrees to pay back what he has stolen. (See verses 8–10.) God is at work in the broken people who cause the broken misery of this world. I think

Zacchaeus paying back those he wronged represents God working to bring restoration to those who have suffered, be it through others in this life or ultimately in His kingdom. The banquet at Zacchaeus's house is a wonderful story that illustrates how Christ makes all things new, both in the manipulated and in the manipulator.

The eighth meal scene takes place on the night of the Passover when Jesus speaks to His disciples about His work on the cross. (See Luke 22:7–38.) He urges His disciples to serve those who are least among them. (See verses 26–27.) Because of God's work on the cross, the least will be served, and their suffering not forgotten.

In the ninth meal scene (Luke 24:13–35), Jesus has risen from the dead. He appears to Cleopas and another disciple, but they do not know who Christ is. They tell Him that they expected Jesus of Nazareth to fix the broken system in Israel (see verse 21), but He has been crucified. They have a meal together and, during this meal, Jesus opens their eyes. These two men represent those who are looking in all the wrong places as they seek God to bring restoration to the suffering. It's not until we understand God's table that we realize He's been at work in the suffering. Suffering will not be ended by another political movement. It will be over at the table to which Christ calls us, where all partake of Him and are content.

Finally, in the last meal scene (Luke 24:36–53), Jesus appears to His disciples who have disowned Him in His suffering. Jesus does the most intimate thing He could do: He shares a meal with them. He opens up His table to them. He shows that His kingdom is open to those who have turned their backs on God.

The ten meal scenes are a wink in Luke's gospel. This world is full of broken systems, with manipulators winning and the manipulated losing. And here in this fallen world, full of its systems, the Lord Jesus calls both the manipulator and the manipulated to His table. He presides and reconciles the afflicted to the afflicter. He conquers evil through giving of Himself.

To everyone who aches because they are sick, rejected by the system, orphaned, abandoned, unsure about God, overlooked, condemned as a criminal, or considered a reprobate, God has issued an invitation His kingdom, where He has given of Himself. The banquet table of the Lord has some very unusual guests. When you wonder what God is doing about the suffering of those who have been the prey of society and the suffering caused by those who have been the curse of society, just remember the meal scenes in Luke. God winks at His banquet table. He has prepared His kingdom with them in mind.

Wink #23

GOD WINKS IN THE FOILS

Characters are extremely important to any story, especially biblical narratives. Think about it for a moment. The biblical writers never sat down and told us fact after fact about Jesus. Matthew didn't list the top ten things about Jesus's humanity. Mark didn't give us five points about the Trinity. Luke didn't offer us pointers on Jesus's divinity. John didn't give us any theological treatises about Christ's take on human suffering. Instead, they told their theology in story form. The account of Christ is storied theology—theology that emerges from the story.

As good readers of the New Testament narratives, we shouldn't toss the story to get at the theology. Too often, biblical readers come to the story, trying to find points for sermons and statements to build theological arguments while discarding the storytelling elements. But we should appreciate the story for the story's sake.

One way that rich observations emerge is through the characters in the story. Where are they introduced? Whom do they speak with? What is unique about them? Why are they in the story? This is called characterization, how a character develops in a story. Paying attention to how a character develops offers us some pleasant surprises. These give us subtle winks that flood our spiritual senses with an awareness of God's heart toward humankind.

PAYING ATTENTION TO HOW A CHARACTER DEVELOPS OFFERS US SUBTLE WINKS THAT FLOOD OUR SPIRITUAL SENSES WITH AN AWARENESS OF GOD'S HEART TOWARD HUMANKIND.

There are different categories of characters within stories. One of the characters we meet is known as a *foil*, someone who is placed in the story to emphasize something about another character. Just as a shiny sheet of foil is placed next to a jewel to enhance its brilliance, foils are included in a story to enhance other characters.

An example of a modern-day foil would be Buzz Lightyear in *Toy Story*. He enhances our concept of Woody. At first, Woody seems like a congenial type. All the toys like him. It isn't until Buzz Lightyear comes into the story that Woody's jealous and manipulative sides are revealed. Buzz brings this out for the audience to see.

In the New Testament narratives, there are several foils. We will look at four that give us a wink about what God is doing about the suffering of those in the margins.

The first foil is the poor widow in Mark 12:41–44. Before she shows up, the rich are seen giving large sums of money to the temple treasury. It seems noble. Impressive. When the marginalized woman enters, she gives two small copper coins—the smallest coins in circulation. Jesus points out that this is *all* the woman had to give. It was her life savings.

Suddenly, there is a twist in the scene. Her giving puts the spotlight on the rich who gave. It makes their gift seem self-protective, even self-centered. The tables have turned. The reader must stop and think now: who actually is serving God? Who is part of His kingdom? The Lord does not honor the pretentious rich but the poor. God has made a place for them in His kingdom.

The second foil we find are the women at the cross in John 19:25. John makes a special point to say they were present. In doing so, the women act as a foil, illuminating who was *not* there: Jesus's disciples. In a culture that valued the courage and bravery of men, women are the ones portrayed as heroic. Most of the disciples were hiding in terror, in fear for their lives. But the women were on the front lines.

As we have already noted, it was unthinkable for women to be considered disciples in Bible times. Yet, they were superior disciples of Jesus in His most crucial hour. The brave and loyal characterization of these three women says something for women who found themselves in the margins of that society.

The oppressive Roman culture has placed Jesus on the cross. It had also suppressed His women followers up to that point. In His crucifixion, He overcomes His followers' suffering. Through their unrelenting faith, they share in His triumph over suffering caused by the culture's oppression, freeing them to be His unashamed, bold followers.

The third foil is the centurion soldier in Mark 15:39, whom we examined in chapter 4. During Christ's crucifixion, the centurion chimes in and says, *"Truly this man was the Son of God!"* This is quite an amazing statement. This is the first time in Mark's gospel that a human confesses that Jesus is the Son of God.

The centurion is the last person we would expect to say this. Centurions were known for their barbaric, lawless lifestyles. The hardened heart of the centurion was softened by the suffering death he witnessed in the Messiah's crucifixion. This acts as a foil toward the Jewish religious leaders who were present. The suffering of Jesus didn't move them. It only hardened their hearts further. What a contrast. A sinful gentile is moved by the death of Jesus, but the high priest of Israel is not.

The characterization of the centurion speaks to the place that gentiles have in the kingdom of God. Though the religious leaders had considered gentiles unclean, the Scripture tells us there is room for them in God's family. The Romans would later destroy Jerusalem and slaughter many Jews. The fact that the narrative tells us that God was working within the Roman army is significant. God was already at work in Israel's opponents. Christ had begun reconciling oppressor to the oppressed through His death on the cross.

The tormentor and the tormented come together in Jesus, where they find redemption and restitution. Through the characters at the cross, namely the centurion foil, God winks and shows how His death is solving the problem of suffering and bringing together those at the margins.

The last foil we will examine is the Canaanite woman in Matthew 15:21–28. She is a gentile whose daughter is oppressed by a demon. She comes to Jesus and asks Him to heal her daughter. Her faith is so strong that Jesus commends her, saying, *"O woman, great is your faith!"* (verse 28). She is a foil placed next to the Pharisees.

Throughout Matthew, the Pharisees suppose that Jesus is a messianic phony. By placing the gentile woman next to the Pharisees, Matthew shows that a gentile woman on the sidelines can have more faith in Christ than those who are zealous and religious. She was the wrong kind of person with the right kind of faith. This shows her place in Christ's kingdom.

THE FOILS WE SEE IN THE GOSPELS ARE SUBTLE INTIMATIONS THAT SHOW GOD AT WORK IN THE SUFFERING OF THE MARGINALIZED.

In each characterization, God winks. The foils we see are subtle intimations that show God at work in the suffering of the marginalized. These unsuspecting characters we meet in the text give us a big reminder: Jesus is doing something about the sorrow of this broken world with its broken systems. He's at work.

The victories these unsuspecting individuals stumble upon show that God's providence is guiding the weak into His family to experience restoration, redemption, and the recovery of all things that a sinful world has stolen.

Though all of God's providence is not realized in the here and now, the stories of these subtle characters give us hope that God hasn't overlooked those the world has snubbed. Where is God when we see people in the world oppressing and suffering oppression? God winks in the foils. The system may have left the weak behind, but God hasn't. He knows the faith of those who appear small. This small faith brings these individuals into a big kingdom where evil and suffering have been defeated.

Wink #24

GOD WINKS IN HIS PROVISION

God is our provider. From the first chapter of Genesis, when God placed Adam into Eden, through the last chapters of Revelation, where the city of God comes down from heaven to the new earth, God tends to His creation. God is humankind's ultimate sustenance. This is one of the grand narratives in Scripture.

This is especially important to remember in times of suffering. God does not cease being our provider when we experience sorrow, tragedy, or loss. He sustains us through these crises. Hard as it may be to comprehend, He is there. He is enough. The apostle Paul alludes to this during his great sufferings, saying, *"And my God will supply every need of yours according to his riches in glory in Christ Jesus"* (Philippians 4:19).

When he wrote to the church at Philippi, Paul was under house arrest as a prisoner of Rome. The apostle had been through great trials and was headed for more. He had already told the church that he was a participant in Christ's sufferings. (See Philippians 1:29–30; 3:8–10.) So, when Paul says that God will meet every need, he was suggesting that God meets every need while we are suffering, not apart from it. Paul did not see God's grace as being apart from the sufferings he was enduring. The two went together in the apostle's mind. (See 2 Corinthians 12:9.)

God's grace is no different for those of us who suffer today. Whether it is suffering because of marginalization, loss, a heart-breaking circumstance, or some other cause, we can expect God's grace to meet us in the form of *provision* in these trials. The Gospel of Luke winks at us. It subtly prompts us to trust God as *sustainer* during our suffering.

NO MATTER HOW OR WHY WE ARE SUFFERING, WE CAN EXPECT GOD'S GRACE TO MEET US IN THE FORM OF PROVISION IN THESE TRIALS.

One of the main purposes of Luke's gospel is to show that God's promises to His suffering people are fulfilled in Jesus the Messiah. Therefore, there are many instances in Luke in which the Messiah's power is put on display. One of these occurs when Jesus feeds the multitudes in Luke 9:10–17. It's easy to get excited about the miracle in this story and not catch the nuances behind its significance. However, in the story's subtle nuances, we find a wink. In order to see it, we need to pay attention to where the story is placed, in the third pericope in Luke 9. A pericope is a set of verses that contain a complete unit of thought.

In the first one, Jesus sends out the disciples to preach. He tells them to take nothing with them on their journeys. (See Luke 9:1–6.) Following this, in the next pericope, Herod is perplexed. He is told about all the miracles of Jesus, and some tell him that Elijah has appeared. (See verses 7–9.) After these two pericopes, we see the pericope where Jesus feeds the multitudes, and the disciples pick up twelve baskets of leftovers. (See verses 10–17.) Following this, in the fourth pericope, Jesus asks His disciples who people are saying He is. Peter tells Him that some say He is Elijah, but Peter also admits that He is the Christ. (See verses 18–20.)

Four different stories. But whether you realize it or not, they are all cleverly connected. How? It appears in how they are arranged. I am using A and B to show how I believed Luke organized them and how they should be understood:

+ A1. Jesus sends the disciples out and tells them to take nothing. (Verses 1–6)

  » B1. Herod is perplexed. Some tell him Jesus might be Elijah. (Verses 7–9)

+ A2. Jesus feeds the multitudes, and the disciples pick up twelve baskets of leftovers. (Verses 10–17)

  » B2. Peter tells Jesus that people think He is Elijah, but Peter says He is the Christ. (Verses 18–20)

The arrangement of these pericopes tells us more than is explicitly stated in the story.

First let's examine the B group. In B1, Herod is perplexed. Some are telling him Elijah has appeared. In B2, Peter tells Jesus about this chatter.

Why would people even think that Jesus was Elijah? As readers, we *know* He isn't Elijah. But imagine living back then. Luke takes full advantage of the people's superstition.

How? Luke inserts A2 between the chatter in B1 and B2. Why? A little detail in A2 connects them: Jesus tells the disciples to have the multitudes *"sit down in groups of about fifty each"* (verse 14). Why groups of fifty? Why not groups of thirty? Or one hundred?

Fifty was a key number. In 1 Kings 18:13, Obadiah tells Elijah that he supplied food and water to one hundred of God's prophets during a time of famine when Ahab and Jezebel wanted to kill them all. The prophets were arranged into two groups of fifty. This story is echoed when Jesus arranges the division of the multitudes into groups of fifty. It would, quite naturally, bring Elijah to mind.

Imagine living back then and seeing Jesus do this. You might be tempted to consider the possibility that Jesus is Elijah. This would have been exciting because, as in Elijah's day, God's people were under trial and experienced great suffering. They were oppressed by the Romans, afflicted with disease, plagued by demons, and marginalized by the religious elites. Life was hard.

Yet this Jesus, whoever He was, was feeding God's people in their suffering. Elijah or not, He was working in their pain. He was demonstrating that His work was similar to the times of Elijah by having the people sit in groups of fifty. He was proving to be the source of sustenance.

Great, right? There's more. What does A1, the pericope where Jesus sends His disciples out and tells them to take nothing with them, have to do with this? This, too, is revealed in A2.

In A2, we are told this Elijah-like figure fed everyone until they were satisfied. (See Luke 9:17.) So much so, in fact, that the disciples picked up *"twelve baskets"* of food. Twelve is not a coincidental number. There was a basketful for each disciple—each disciple Jesus had sent out after telling them to take nothing with them. Now it makes sense. Not only did this Elijah-like figure provide for the masses, but He also provided for His close followers. He gives the masses what they need in their broken-world suffering, and He gives His disciples what they need in the suffering they experience as His disciples.

So, was the mystery man Elijah or not?

Luke breaks the suspense in B2. No, He is greater than Elijah. Peter reveals that the mystery man is Jesus, the Messiah. He is the sustainer of His creation in times of suffering, sorrow, and trial. Where is God at in our pain? He's in us, providing for us, whether we realize it or not. He is the source of our sustenance.

We don't have the answer for everyone's suffering, that's for sure. There's no way that we can account for some of the deepest suffering. Perhaps it's a bit oversimplistic, but something in these pericopes suggests that the Messiah satisfies those who cannot satisfy themselves. He will accomplish this in this life or in the kingdom to come. I do believe those who have been shortchanged in this life by the brokenness of sin will come to see that the Messiah has prepared for their sustenance nonetheless. They have a basketful waiting for them. God is not negligent.

> THOSE WHO HAVE BEEN SHORTCHANGED IN THIS LIFE BY THE BROKENNESS OF SIN WILL COME TO SEE THAT THE MESSIAH HAS PREPARED FOR THEIR SUSTENANCE NONETHELESS.

The pericopes in this story teach us to trust the Messiah while things are coming together. Though it seems uncertain where God is in the realm of human sorrow, the world will come to see that God has been at work in their midst the entire time, even if they didn't realize He was there.

He subtly winks in His provision. The source of our sustenance has been arranging a basketful for all who have suffered at the hands of this world, for all those left with nothing.

Wink #25

GOD WINKS IN OUR RESCUE

God is not only our provider in times of suffering, He is also our rescuer. In the biblical narrative, God shows Himself strong through mighty works to rescue His people in peril.

The story of the early church in Acts is full of these instances. From the moment the Spirit is poured out, the young believers find themselves in harm's way. The apostles are persecuted, jailed, beaten, and stoned. Some are left for dead. In many instances, God saves them from their oppressors and gives them the strength to carry on.

The tricky thing is that this is not always the case. Acts gives us a mixed bag. Some disciples are killed, and there is no apparent rescue. Some disciples are let off the hook while others are not. There is tension. This becomes obvious as the reader works through the narrative.

An example of this tension is found in Acts 12. Here we find that the disciple James has been killed by Herod. (See verse 2.) The fact that he killed James with the sword suggests that Herod saw the growing church as a political threat. Killing a disciple was

184 WINKS FROM SCRIPTURE

a means of intimidation and an attempt to halt the church by eliminating its leadership.

The next disciple on the chopping block was Peter. (See verse 3.) Herod gave the order to have Peter arrested and imprisoned. It would be logical for Peter to assume that his fate would be the same as James's. Peter, John, and James, John's brother, were part of Jesus's inner circle. (See Matthew 17:1.) Anyone reading this story for the first time could reasonably assume that Peter would die, too.

At this point, Luke, who is the writer of Acts, offers a detail that changes where the story seems to head. It enhances the suspense. Luke says that Peter was put into prison during Passover. (See Acts 12:3.) This is sincerely a subtle wink of irony.

Just as Peter was imprisoned, the Jewish people were celebrating how God rescued their people from the hand of the wicked Pharaoh. Is this a coincidental detail? Not in the least. Luke is signaling a plot twist. Peter's fate deviates from the fate of James.

An angel of the Lord appears and awakens Peter. The chains fall off of the apostle's hands. The angel tells Peter to get dressed and follow him, so Peter follows the angel past two guards to a gate, which miraculously opens. At that point, Peter realizes he isn't dreaming. He's been rescued. (See Acts 12:7–11.) Not the same outcome as James, that's for sure.

The language that Luke uses to tell this story might even be more interesting than the story itself. Luke says Herod "laid *violent* hands on some who belonged to the church" (Acts 12:1). In the Greek Septuagint, this word "violent" (*kakos*) is used to describe the evil that Pharaoh was doing to the Hebrews. (See Exodus 3:7.) This creates a subtle link between Pharaoh and Herod. With this, the persecution of the church is being compared to the persecution of the Hebrew slaves in Egypt.

When Peter is rescued, he says, *"Now I am sure that the Lord has sent his angel and **rescued** me from the hand of Herod and from all that the Jewish people were expecting"* (Acts 12:11).

The word "rescue" (*exaireō*) is the same word used by the Greek Septuagint when God tells Moses He has come to *deliver* or *rescue* the Hebrew people from Egypt. (See Exodus 3:8.) Furthermore, Peter tells those at the home of Mary how God "brought" (*exagō*) him out of prison. (See Acts 12:17.) This is the same word used in the Greek Septuagint when God tells Moses He is going to bring the children of Israel out of Egypt into the promised land. (See Exodus 3:8.)

> THE LANGUAGE USED IN ACTS 12 SHOWS US THAT THE GOD WHO MIRACULOUSLY DELIVERED THE HEBREWS IN EXODUS IS THE SAME GOD WHO IS AT WORK IN THE EARLY CHURCH.

All of this language links the events of the Passover in Acts 12 to the first Passover in Exodus. It winks, showing that the God who miraculously delivered the Hebrews is the same God who is at work in the early church. The God of the Hebrews is the God of the Christians, now revealed in Jesus Christ and at work through the Holy Spirit. He's a rescuer, and He rescues Peter.

And yet we cannot forget about the one element in this story that makes it a conundrum.

James.

James didn't have the same outcome as the Hebrew people or Peter. There was no rescue. There was no parade out of prison nor a warm reception at the home of people who loved him. Instead, a sword perforated his guts.

How do we make sense of this? What are we supposed to make of this in a story that has clearly alluded that God is a mighty deliverer? Where was God in James's case? Is James's outcome inconsistent and out of place?

I don't think so. I think the tension is finely placed. Once again, we are left to probe the mystery of the dark night with our questions, questions that will never get us any closer to knowing *why*, only closer to knowing *Him*. Sometimes there are spectacular deliverances; sometimes there is silence and a sword through the stomach. God's rescue in the here and now is mysteriously linked to His sovereignty.

Yet, the tension does more. It helps us to understand God as our rescuer, despite the outcome His sovereignty allows for in our earthly lives. God is our rescuer, and that doesn't change when He chooses not to rescue in the here-and-now. For instance, although God delivers Peter from prison in Acts 12, history tells us that Peter dies hanging upside down on a cross. Did God cease to be a rescuer? No. God's ultimate deliverance takes place when He brings Peter into His eternal kingdom. Paul affirms this shortly before his own death:

> **The Lord will rescue me** *from every evil deed and bring me safely into his heavenly kingdom. To him be the glory forever and ever. Amen.* (2 Timothy 4:18)

Any rescue that God performs now only points to the ultimate rescue that is to come.

Was He the Hebrew slaves' rescuer? Yes. Was He Peter's rescuer? Yes. Was He James's rescuer? Ultimately, yes, He was. Is He ours? No matter the outcome, there is no doubt that He *is* our rescuer. The narrative in Scripture winks. In times of uncertain suffering, we can be certain that He has secured our rescue—however and whenever it comes.

Wink #26

GOD WINKS IN THE EXODUS

Our view of God is challenged as we wrestle with the mystery of suffering. Who is God to broken humanity, living in a fallen world, shrouded in darkness? Luke knows this question. In Acts, he portrays God as a rescuer, which we saw in the previous study.

But this isn't an anomaly for Luke. He does this in other places. He tells the story of Jesus in his gospel using the same strategy. In doing so, he gives a wink and reinforces the idea that we should see God as rescuer to a creation that's in the clutches of evil and sin.

One thing I always tell my New Testament students is that if they see only one story while reading the narratives, they need to dig deeper. The New Testament narratives are always kicking back to Old Testament histories and echoing them because the gospel writers believed that Jesus was part of Israel's story. The things He did resemble the things Israel's prophets did. As a result, the things that happen in the Gospels are strikingly similar to Old Testament narratives—only better because Jesus is the Messiah.

CERTAIN WORDS, PHRASES, SETTINGS, EVENTS, AND MIRACLES IN THE GOSPELS ECHO THE OLD TESTAMENT, LETTING US KNOW THAT WE HAVE ONE GOD THROUGHOUT THE BIBLE.

Understanding this, New Testament narratives should make you think of the Old Testament. There should be moments when you are reading and realize, "This story sounds familiar." Certain words, phrases, settings, events, and miracles should trigger this thinking. These *echoes* are links that add layers of meaning and theological value to the story. They show that we have one God throughout the Bible, that Christ is the fulfilment of Old Testament expectations, and that God has been working throughout human history to deliver humankind from the problem of evil and suffering.

Echoes can be fully observed in Luke's gospel. In a several instances, Luke places echoes to call readers back to Exodus events. Doing so places Christ's story side by side with the story of Moses. These echoes are subtle winks. If we catch them, we will enhance our picture of Christ as the rescuer of oppressed creation.

The first wink comes in Zechariah's prophecy. (See Luke 1:67–79.) Zechariah begins by saying, "*Blessed be the Lord God of Israel, for he has **visited and redeemed his people**"* (verse 68). God's ultimate visitation for His people in the Old Testament came at the exodus. By using visitation language, Luke sets the stage for the coming of the Messiah. Luke builds suspense. Readers start to suspect another deliverer is coming.

The next wink is found in Luke 8:22–25. In this story, the disciples and Jesus are in a boat on the Sea of Galilee. The wind stirs up the waves, and water spills into the boat. Frightened, the disciples wake up Jesus and urge Him to act. Jesus rebukes the wind and the churning waters. The sea calms down. This action echoes Moses, who controlled the wind and waves of the Red Sea.

(See Exodus 14:21–22.) It confirms Jesus is another deliverer, like Moses.

Later, in Luke 9:10–17, Jesus feeds the suffering multitudes with five loaves of bread and two fish. This spectacular event echoes God's provision for the Israelites in the wilderness under the leadership of Moses. (See Exodus 16.) It winks that God, in Christ, is God's plan of provision and deliverance for His suffering people.

In Luke 9:28–36, we find the story of Christ's transfiguration. Here we find other winks that place Jesus alongside Moses:

+ Jesus goes up on a mountain. (Compare Exodus 19:2–3.)

+ There is clear mention of Moses appearing with Jesus.

+ Jesus's countenance changes. (Compare Exodus 34:29–30.)

+ There is a mention of tents. (Compare Exodus 33:7–11.)

+ A cloud overshadowed the disciples. (Compare Exodus 24:15.)

+ The disciples are afraid. (Compare Exodus 20:18.)

THE DETAILS IN LUKE'S STORY OF CHRIST'S TRANSFIGURATION LINK US BACK TO EXODUS. JESUS IS SET UP AS A RESCUER WHO IS EVEN GREATER THAN MOSES.

Each of these details pertain to specific events that took place during the exodus and the wilderness wanderings. Here we have several places where the story of Jesus is told in comparison with God's great visitation upon the people of Israel in Exodus. Luke sets Jesus up as the rescuer of God's people—a rescuer who is even greater than Moses. It tells us that God has *ultimately* dealt with the problem of evil and suffering in our broken state through the work of the Messiah. The narrative keeps us focused on this.

With this in mind, it is interesting to consider an event in Luke in which Jesus is questioned about human suffering. In Luke 13:1–5, Jesus discusses two tragedies. The first was a violent massacre of Galileans; the second was an accident where a tower had fallen on eighteen people. If either of these had happened today, they would be breaking news. Perhaps we could compare the first event to a mall shooting and the second event to a bridge collapsing.

If there is any place in Scripture where I wish Jesus had said more, it is here. But He doesn't. He offers no theodicy. The Master gives us no comforting answers to explain why these terrible events occurred. Instead, He taps into the emotions they evoked in the local residents. In doing so, He calls them to repentance. By repentance, Jesus is calling the people to shift directions, to disavow their trust in a world where evil tyrants commit murder and buildings fall on people.

To further emphasize this, Jesus tells the parable of the fig tree in the vineyard. (See Luke 13:6–9.) This parable informs us that Jesus has been looking for those who will repent. Will people trust Him as the deliverer from a world full of sorrow? Will those who hear His message believe that He frees them from evil and suffering? If not, they, too, will ultimately become the victims of an evil world.

Jesus keeps His audience's focus on His main purpose, which was to deliver them from evil and sin so He can lead them into His eternal kingdom. Jesus exhorts His audience to repent so that this can take place. That was His emphasis. Other matters pertaining to theodicy seem subordinate.

Readers are left with a challenge: will we disavow the world and follow Christ, though the mystery of suffering remains? Christ can be trusted. The text winks: Jesus is the deliverer. He is the God of the exodus. We can put our hope in Him to lead us out of this broken world. Let us all repent and turn our allegiance to Him.

GOD WINKS IN
GOLDEN OPPORTUNITIES

The book of Acts winks at us. Paul's house arrest in Rome tells us there might be golden opportunities that await.

Golden enterprises are gifts in our suffering. The trials we face bring opportunities we otherwise wouldn't have. While looking for God in our hour of sorrow, it serves us well to suspect Him to be at work in the unique occasions that only suffering can bring. God's providence is never dormant, not even when we're in distress. It's always at work, sometimes even in ways so absurd that we overlook them. The Acts narrative winks and shows us this because the entire book is framed by an inclusio concerned with suffering.

Acts begins with a focus on the preaching of the kingdom despite suffering. The first part of this inclusio is in Acts 1:3, when Jesus *"presented himself alive to them after his suffering by many proofs, appearing to them during forty days and speaking about **the kingdom of God**."* On the other end of that inclusio is the last chapter of Acts, chapter 28. The last verse in the story ends with the apostle Paul teaching what Jesus taught to begin the story in Acts: *"the kingdom of God."*

At this point, Paul was on house arrest as a prisoner of Rome. He had been through floggings, stoning, shipwreck, and imprisonment. But there he was, still preaching the gospel, despite his own suffering, just as Jesus had done.

> *He lived there* [on house arrest in Rome] *two whole years at his own expense, and welcomed all who came to him, proclaiming the kingdom of God and teaching about the Lord Jesus Christ with all boldness and without hindrance.*
>
> (Acts 28:30–31)

The inclusio looks like this:

- Christ preaches the kingdom despite His suffering (Acts 1:3)

  » The book of Acts

- Paul preaches the kingdom despite his suffering (Acts 28:30–31)

THE ENTIRE BOOK OF ACTS IS ABOUT SHARING THE GOSPEL OF THE KINGDOM TO THE NATIONS OF THE EARTH DESPITE GREAT TRIALS AND AFFLICTIONS.

The inclusio is a wink. It gives us a picture of what the entire book of Acts is about: sharing the gospel of the kingdom to the nations of the earth despite great trials and afflictions. Everything in Acts happens between suffering. *The wink signals that despite tribulation, there are opportunities for the kingdom that wouldn't have been possible otherwise.*

For instance, take Paul's house arrest in Acts 28. His situation enabled him to write letters to the churches and preach the gospel to all who came to see him. In fact, during this time, Paul wrote his letter to the Philippian church wherein he declares that his time suffering on house arrest was a *golden opportunity*. He proclaims, *"I want you to know, brothers, that what has happened to me has really served to advance the gospel"* (Philippians 1:12).

Here, Paul is referring to the imperial guard who began to hear about Christ because of Paul's house arrest in Rome. (See Philippians 1:13.) This is *quite* the golden opportunity! The imperial guard was a special class of Roman soldiers who were the emperor's bodyguards. These were nine thousand hardened soldiers and unsympathetic pagans. They were known as *kingmakers* because after they served as Praetorian soldiers, they were granted high honors and achieved political influence. The imperial guard played an important role in choosing the next emperor.

During his house arrest, Paul was shackled to a soldier, separated by eighteen inches of chain. That's quite the providence of God. Before the guards made decisions for the Roman Empire, they had to be chained next to Paul. Ironically, this was a more of a sentence for the imperial guard than it was for Paul! God had sentenced them to hearing the gospel of Jesus. And as Paul informs the church at Philippi, it was effective, an opportunity amidst his suffering.

> DURING HIS HOUSE ARREST, PAUL WAS
> SHACKLED TO A SOLDIER—A GOLDEN
> OPPORTUNITY FOR HIM TO SPREAD
> THE GOSPEL TO THE IMPERIAL GUARD.

Paul could never have set up a plan like this himself. It's too absurd to have been crafted by the mind of man. Our own ideas of providence are too obvious. God's way of providence is more mysterious, requiring us to trust in His grace. God's providence often includes suffering.

So, Acts winks at us. Stories like Paul's house arrest in Rome tell us there might be golden opportunities that await. This is affirmed elsewhere in the Acts narrative.

In one instance, Paul is stoned and dragged out of the city of Lystra and yet he returns there to preach. (See Acts 14:19–21.) He exhorts the church there, telling them, *"Through many tribulations we must enter the kingdom of God"* (verse 22). In a few words, Paul was encouraging the young church not to discard their suffering or see it as irrelevant. Rather, God's providence was at work in the hardships. Paul was encouraging them to see God at work in them, in the suffering. Looking at it that way would help them notice God's subtle wink through a golden opportunity.

The challenge is not to perceive our sufferings merely as assaults. Had Paul understood suffering only that way, he wouldn't have had an ironic testimony for the Philippian church. But Paul noticed God's mysterious and odd providence. Because of this, he accessed the golden opportunity that was there. He made an impression for the kingdom that he might never have imagined.

As we face sorrows in the world and suffering beyond our control, we have to decide how we want to respond. Do we accept suffering as our defeat, or do we see ourselves like those in the book of Acts who saw what God was doing despite their affliction? That takes faith.

Process your trials by comparing them to the trials in Acts. Do you notice opportunities like those? Imagine how Paul must have felt when he was able to tell the imperial guard about Christ. Absurd. Odd. Mysterious. Who could ever have suspected?

There's a chance you'll feel the same when you discover a golden opportunity in your hour of suffering. Who knows what God's providence will bring? In these opportunities, God winks.

Wink #28

GOD WINKS IN ASSURING US
ALL WILL BE WELL

Great Christian minds—people like C. S. Lewis, Augustine of Hippo, and Julian of Norwich—have wrestled with the problem of evil throughout the centuries of Christian history.[12] While they offer profound insights that invite us to draw nearer to the Author of our faith, the one question we would all like to have answered remains a mystery:

Why does God allow evil and suffering?

By now, we've established that this question will *not* be answered—at least not here and not now.

Marilyn McCord Adams, an Anglican theologian, says one reason for this is that humans are "cognitively, emotionally, and/or spiritually too immature" to comprehend the mystery of suffering.[13]

---

12. In this chapter, I draw on the work of Daniel DeForest London, *Theodicy and Spirituality in the Fourth Gospel: A Girardian Perspective* (New York, NY: Lexington Books/Fortress Academic, 2020). While doing my thesis work, I especially appreciated how London drew Lewis, Augustine, and Julian into a conversation to explain the unexplainable nature of theodicy.
13. Marilyn McCord Adams, "Horrendous Evils and the Goodness of God," in *The Problem of Evil*, ed. Marilyn McCord Adams and Robert Merrihew Adams (Oxford, UK: Oxford University Press, 1990), in DeForest London, *Theodicy and Spirituality in the Fourth Gospel*, 11.

Modernity has led us to believe that, with enough empiricism, we can get to the bottom of everything. In other words, there's no mystery that science and reason can't eventually figure out. But Adams reminds us of our limitations as humans. Practicing our faith means accepting mystery. It's trusting God when we don't have an answer, won't have an answer, and *can't* have an answer.

PRACTICING OUR FAITH MEANS ACCEPTING MYSTERY—TRUSTING GOD WHEN WE DON'T HAVE AN ANSWER, WON'T HAVE AN ANSWER, AND CAN'T HAVE AN ANSWER.

C. S. Lewis admits this in my favorite book of his, *A Grief Observed*. While grieving the death of his wife, Joy Davidman, Lewis questions God. He eventually admits:

> When I lay these questions before God I get no answer. But a rather special sort of 'No answer.' It is not the locked door. It is more like a silent, certainly not uncompassionate, gaze. As though He shook His head not in refusal but waiving the question. Like, 'Peace, child: you don't understand.' Can a mortal ask questions which God finds unanswerable? Quite easily, I should think. All nonsense questions are unanswerable. How many hours are there in a mile? Is yellow square or round? Probably half the questions we ask—half our great theological and metaphysical problems—are like that.[14]

No answer for Lewis.

Augustine of Hippo also wrestles with the mystery behind suffering:

---

14. C. S. Lewis, *A Grief Observed* (New York, NY: HarperOne, 2017), 69.

I was seeking feverishly for the origins of evil. What torments my heart suffered in mental pregnancy, what groans, my God! And though I did not know it, your ears were there. As in silence I vigorously pursued my quest, inarticulate sufferings of my heart were loudly pleading for your mercy. You knew what I endured; no human knew. How little of it my tongue could put into words for the ears of my closest friends! Neither the time nor my powers of speech were sufficient to tell them of the full tumult of my soul. But all of it came to your hearing, how I roared from the groaning of my heart, and my desire was before you, and the light of my eyes was not with me.[15]

No answer for Augustine.

Yet there is much to be gained. In an age of "health and wealth" Christianity, where we are told that God is in the prospering, Lewis and Augustine remind us that we discover God when we come to terms with our mortality. God is in our brokenness. It's refreshing to hear God's people come to terms with their humanity instead of shunning it and pretending to be superheroes. There are a lot of roads in this, which lead us to God's heart.

This leaves us trusting the Author of our faith to be the Finisher of our faith and make all things well. That's what Julian of Norwich, the fourteenth-century mystic, concludes in her own examination of evil and suffering:

And after this our Lord brought to my mind the longing I had for him before, and I saw that nothing hindered me but sin, and I saw that this is true of all of us in general, and it seemed to me that if there had been no sin, we should all have been pure and like as our Lord as he created us.

---

15. Augustine of Hippo, *Confessions*, trans. Henry Chadwick (Oxford, UK: Oxford University Press, 1998), VII.7, in DeForest London, *Theodicy and Spirituality in the Fourth Gospel*, 10–11.

And so, in my folly before this time I often wondered why, through the great prescient wisdom of God, the beginning of sin was not prevented. For then it seemed to me that all would have been well…And it seems to me that this pain is something for a time, for it purges and makes us know ourselves and ask for mercy…It is true that sin is the cause of all this pain, *but all will be well, and every kind of thing will be well.*[16]

Julian of Norwich, Augustine, and C. S. Lewis align closer to Scriptures in their approach to suffering and theodicy than those who have apologetic gymnastics to offer. Biblical narratives resist complicated answers to explaining why humans suffer. There's something especially divine about simplicity.

EVIL EXISTS AND SIN CAUSES DEATH, BUT JESUS IS AT WORK TO MAKE ALL THINGS WELL, SO WE SHOULD TRUST HIM.

Evil exists and sin causes death, but Jesus is at work to make all things well, so we should trust Him. It can be said more poetically or more profoundly. We can look at it in different ways using diverse perspectives and methodologies. But that's the bottom line, folks. It's also what Matthew gets at in his telling of the story of Jesus. Using repetition, Matthew winks at us and shares this simple truth.

Nothing tips us off quicker to what an author is getting at than when he repeats a word, phrase, theme, or situation later in his narrative. These repetitions often serve as structural markers that summarize what the author has been saying. Matthew does this to

---

16. Julian of Norwich, *Julian of Norwich: Showings*, ed. Richard J. Payne, trans. Edmund Colledge and James Walsh, *The Classics of Western Spirituality* (Mahwah, NJ: Paulist Press, 1978), 225. (Emphasis mine.)

assure our finite minds that God, through Christ, is making sure that all shall be well.

To see this, we begin at Matthew 4:23, where he tells us that Jesus *"went throughout all Galilee, teaching in their synagogues and proclaiming the gospel of the kingdom and healing every disease and every affliction among the people."*

In Matthew 9:35, Matthew states again:

And Jesus went throughout all the cities and villages, teaching in their synagogues and proclaiming the gospel of the kingdom and healing every disease and every affliction.

This repetitive statement lets us know that Matthew is doing something intentional here. If we examine the passages between each statement, we will discover what that is.

Matthew 4:23 comes right before Jesus gives His most profound sermon of all time, the Sermon on the Mount. (See Matthew 5:1–7:29.) Three whole chapters of Matthew's gospel contain the core of Jesus's teaching.

Immediately after this, Matthew gives us the account of Jesus's healing and miracle ministry that stretches through two chapters and contains ten accounts.

Miracle/Healing	Chapter/verses
Jesus heals a leper	8:1–4
Jesus heals a centurion's servant	8:5–13
Jesus heals Peter's mother-in-law of fever, casts out many demons, and heals all the sick	8:14–17
Jesus calms a raging storm	8:23–27
Jesus delivers two demon-possessed men	8:28–34
Jesus heals a paralytic	9:1–8
Jesus heals a woman with an issue of blood	9:20–22
Jesus raises a ruler's daughter from the dead	9:23–26

Miracle/Healing	Chapter/verses
Jesus heals two blind men	9:27–31
Jesus delivers a deaf mute from a demon	9:32–34

We find Matthew 9:35 right after these accounts. In sequence, Matthew 4:23–9:35 looks like this:

And he went throughout all Galilee, teaching in their synagogues and proclaiming the gospel of the kingdom and healing every disease and every affliction among the people.	Matthew 4:23
The Sermon on the Mount	Matthew 5–7
Jesus's healing/miracle ministry	Matthew 8–9
And Jesus went throughout all the cities and villages, teaching in their synagogues and proclaiming the gospel of the kingdom and healing every disease and every affliction.	Matthew 9:35

By looking at it this way, it becomes apparent what the gospel writer is doing. His first statement in Matthew 4:23 introduces the Lord's teaching ministry as well as His healing and miracle ministry. Then he goes into detail and relates what Christ was teaching, how He was healing, and the miracles He performed in Matthew 5:1–9:34. Finally, Matthew 9:35 repeats the earlier statement to summarize everything.

THE REPETITIVE STATEMENTS IN MATTHEW 4:23 AND 9:35 REINFORCE THE MESSAGE THAT THE TEACHING, HEALING, AND MIRACULOUS MINISTRIES OF JESUS WERE PART OF CHRIST'S MESSIANIC MISSION.

The repetitive statements in Matthew 4:23 and 9:35 form an inclusio that links the events. It is a subtle find, but it serves as a wink. It reinforces the message that the teaching, healing, and miraculous ministries of Jesus were part of Christ's messianic mission. The Messiah joined us in our suffering. He has been active in our pain. He solves our sin, sickness, sorrow, and grief. Amidst it all, He invites us to follow Him into the way of the kingdom. Matthew's use of repetition drives home the idea that the Messiah and His kingdom are God's solution to suffering. And this solution has been implemented.

He's *done* something about our pain, and He's *doing* something about our pain. Because of this, we can rest assured that Scripture is winking at us, and Julian of Norwich was right. *All will be well, and every kind of thing will be well.*

Until that final moment when God wipes away the last tear (see Revelation 21:4), we must trust that God is at work in Christ, despite our inability to understand. This begins by accepting our finitude, owning our brokenness, and placing them into the hands of the One of who *does* have all the answers.

GOD WINKS IN THE WATERS

Does the ocean intimidate you? How about a powerful waterfall or a mighty river? Water is spellbinding. We watch shows on National Geographic about tsunamis. We sit on the beach and stare into the ocean for hours. We get lost in its mystery. We're intrigued by its secrets. Water is enigmatic.

As a native Michigander, I know a little something about water. My home state is surrounded by the Great Lakes. I've spent summers boating on Lake Michigan and walleye fishing on Lake Erie. There's no place I'd rather be—that is, unless the water is angry.

The last time I was at Lake Superior, I thought about the wreckage of the SS *Edmund Fitzgerald*, which sank after getting caught in a fierce storm in November 1975. The entire crew of twenty-nine men perished. At one point, the *Edmund Fitzgerald* was the largest ship to sail the Great Lakes. When it was discovered at the bottom of Lake Superior, the majestic boat was found in two pieces. Looking out at the vast lake—which is really an inland sea—I pondered what it might have been like on that fateful night

when the crew entered the deep, never to emerge again. Such tragedy. Such suffering. Such chaos.

The characteristics of water illustrate the nature of life. Life is
chaotic and mysterious. It seems ordered and beautiful...until it
swallows you up and offers no apology nor gives explanation. You
can't plumb its depths. You don't know what it's hiding. It certainly
will never tell you all its riddles. We love staring out at the sea
because, in doing so, we are staring at the mystery of life. We are
confronted by the paradox of beauty and turmoil, order and disorder, happiness and suffering. The human condition is attracted to
this. Perhaps this is why, when we look out at the sea, we look to
our Creator and yearn for answers.

 THE BOOK OF JOHN REPEATEDLY ALLUDES
TO THE ENIGMATIC NATURE OF WATER.
IT DOESN'T GIVE US ALL OF THE ANSWERS,
BUT IT DOES LET US KNOW THAT GOD IS
SOMEWHERE OUT THERE.

God knows this about us. The book of John repeatedly alludes
to the enigmatic nature of water. It gives us winks in the water.
In fashion with the sea, it doesn't give us all of the answers, but it
does let us know that God is somewhere out there. He's amidst the
mystery, among the chaos, working for our good. It reassures us
that nothing is outside of God's control, as disorderly as the world
may seem to be.

Before looking at the Gospel of John, it's helpful to look at
another book that the apostle John wrote, the book of Revelation.
In Revelation 21:1, John says, "*Then I saw a new heaven and a new
earth, for first heaven and the first earth had passed away, and the sea
was no more.*"

While some understand *"the sea was no more"* to be a literal statement, the apocalyptic genre of Revelation likely suggests this is representational. What could the sea represent? We notice that the sea is often a negative concept in Revelation. The beast rises from the sea (13:1), those who conquer the beast stand beside the sea (15:2), and the sea is linked with Death and Hades (20:13). All of this suggests that the sea symbolizes a place where evil operates, a place in which Satan and his demons function. It's cryptic, eerie, and ominous.

This is not the first time that we see an ominous, evil sea in Scripture. The second verse of the Bible introduces us to a world in chaos, which is indicated by the water that covered it. (See Genesis 1:2.) From the outset of the biblical narrative, water goes hand in hand with a chaotic world surrounded by mysterious darkness. Yet throughout the rest of Genesis 1, God performs a restorative work. He scatters the darkness, He drives back the waters, and He brings forth life out of the chaos. The disarray passes away. God calls this "good."

JOHN SHOWS VARIOUS INSTANCES OF JESUS'S MINISTRY THAT CENTER ON WATER, GIVING US A SUBTLE ECHO BACK TO THE GENESIS ACCOUNT.

The Gospel of John portrays God doing the same thing. God is at work once again, through Jesus the Messiah, bringing the earth from out of chaos as the re-creator. John hints at this by showing various instances of Jesus's ministry that center on water. These are a subtle echo back to the Genesis account. Readers don't usually notice this at first glance. But have a look:

Event in Gospel of John	Verses	Use of Water
Baptism of Jesus	1:32–33	Ministry of Jesus begins in water
First Miracle of Jesus	2:6–10	Jesus turns water into wine
Nicodemus comes to Jesus	3:5	Jesus teaches about being *"born of water and the Spirit"*
Samaritan woman meets Jesus at the well	4:1–15	Jesus teaches about living water
Invalid meets Jesus at the pool of Bethesda	5:1–9	Invalid tells Jesus he has no one to put him in the pool
Jesus walks on water	6:16–21	Jesus walks on the sea in the midst of a storm
Jesus at Feast of Tabernacles	7:37–38	Jesus teaches about living water
A blind man meets Jesus	9:1–7	Jesus spits on the ground, makes mud with saliva, anoints the man's eyes, and tells him to go wash in the pool of Siloam.
The Last Supper	13:5	Jesus washes disciples' feet with water
The crucifixion	19:34	A soldier pierces Jesus's side, and blood and water come out

How does all this water theologize?

John 1:1–5 presents Jesus as the Creator. As Messiah, He brings order to the chaos. The references to water confirm that His work accomplishes this.

+ The baptism in water demonstrates that His ministry is at work in the waters.

+ The miracle of changing water into wine demonstrates that He inaugurates the kingdom from out of the waters.

+ The teaching of being *"born of water and the Spirit"* confirms our need to be cleansed of sin and have our hearts transformed by the Spirit. (Compare Ezekiel 36:25–27.)

+ The explanation to the Samaritan woman teaches us that Jesus offers life-giving water.

+ The healing of the invalid without putting him in the pool demonstrates that Jesus does not need the waters; the waters need Him.

+ Jesus walking on the water demonstrates His authority over the waters.

+ At the Feast of Tabernacles, Jesus declares that those who believe in Him will be filled to overflowing with the *"living water"* of the Holy Spirit.

+ Sending the blind man into the water for healing shows Christ's ability to bring healing from out of the waters.

+ Christ's washing the disciples' feet shows Him blessing His people from the water.

+ The water that comes from His side at the crucifixion shows that the waters were affected by His death.

Hence, in Christ, we see the reworking of the waters, bringing about something life-giving from them. In Genesis 1, God scattered the darkness, drove back the waters, and brought forth new life from out of the deep. All of this is "good."

Interestingly enough, despite this, the Gospel of John does not account for all of our suffering and the chaos in humankind. It offers no theodicy. There are still a thousand and one questions.

But John does assure us that Jesus is in those questions. He is bringing about redemption through the chaos.

That is the answer the text offers. This is what we are invited to focus on. Christ is Lord over the water. The water does what He says. He brings blessings from it and inaugurates His kingdom in it. Because of His restorative work, there will come a day when there is no more disorder, no more suffering, no more evil, and no more mysterious sea.

The Scripture winks. When we stare into the enigmatic waters of mystery and chaos, we can *at least* know, amidst the suffering and sadness out there, that God is out there as well. We hope in this. We *trust* in this.

God Wink #30

GOD WINKS IN THE UNKNOWN

We all have to know how a story ends. We crave certainty. Unless a movie is truly awful, no one would ever leave the theater without knowing how it turns out. It's not well with our soul unless we know what happens.

I'm sure you can relate when you consider your favorite TV show. Have you ever been so into a series that you binge it because you *must* know if the main character lives happily ever after? Perhaps you've raced to the theater restroom after a movie because you've spent two hours drinking a forty-ounce soda but held it in because you couldn't miss the plot twist at the end.

Most of us living in the twenty-first century have been there before. The end satisfies us with what we need most today: answers and certainty. It is part of human nature. Who wants to live not knowing?

Take *The Lion King*, for example. Part of the reason this animated movie is so well-liked is because of its conclusion: Simba gathers his courage and returns to Pride Rock as the rightful king. He overthrows his evil Uncle Scar. He and Nala reign together, have a cub, and Rafiki takes the baby lion and presents him as the next heir. Justice prevails. The kingly lineage is preserved. Order replaces chaos. Everything is the way it should be. As Julian of Norwich put it, "All will be well, and every kind of thing will be well." The end.

But the ending of the HBO hit television show *The Sopranos* in 2007 was not as clear-cut. Twelve million fans tuned in to see what would happen to Tony, his family, and his crew. Would Tony get whacked? The suspense builds until the last scene where Tony is in a diner with his family. His daughter is on the way, arriving late. While Tony, his wife, and his son chitchat at the table, a mysterious man enters. He looks suspicious.

Is he there to kill Tony? Would this be what Tony had coming to him? Suddenly, his daughter arrives. She walks through the door. Tony looks up. The screen goes black. And the show is over.

Nobody, to this day, knows what happened. Did Tony get shot by the mysterious man? Did they all simply live on? Regardless, fans were devastated. My brother and his buddies, longtime fans of the show, agonized for weeks over how it ended. "Why would they leave it this way?" they groaned. They wanted answers. Certainty. It could not be left to their imagination. Someone needed to assure them that Tony and his family were all right. Someone needed to assure them that *all is well, and every kind of thing has been made well.*

In much the same way, we place our expectation for answers and certainty upon Scripture. Sometimes in the text, it meets us with assurance. Yet in other places, Scripture seems more like the conclusion to *The Sopranos*. We're left to wonder, *How does the story end?*

 AFTER NEARLY TWO THOUSAND YEARS, SCHOLARS ARE NOT CERTAIN HOW THE GOSPEL OF MARK REALLY ENDS.

Such is the case with the Gospel of Mark. After nearly two thousand years, scholars are not certain how it really ends. Does it conclude with Mark 16:8 or Mark 16:20? Some of the earliest manuscripts don't include verses 9–20. New Testament scholar Mark Strauss says, "The best textual tradition stops with Mark 16:8. Inferior traditions add 16:9–20."[17]

As the years have passed, I am more convinced it ends at verse 8. Those concerned that any theology may be lost if verses 9–20 are removed should rest assured that every matter of theology covered there can be found elsewhere in Scripture. Nothing is lost.

Mark 16:8 tells us that Mary Magdalene, Mary the mother of James, and Salome *"went out and fled from the tomb, for trembling and astonishment had seized them, and they said nothing to anyone, for they were afraid."* Full stop and on to Luke.

What an abrupt and peculiar ending. It just cuts off with three women in shock after seeing an angel in the tomb of Jesus and hearing him proclaim that the Lord has risen. How can the story end this way?

Yet, Mark's abrupt ending is clever. It is a wink. It does more than a nice, clean, and certain ending could do for us.

The uncertainty of the ending raises several questions for the reader. Where is Jesus? What is He doing at this point? When is He going to appear in Galilee? Why does He want to meet them in Galilee? Why can't He meet them now? Why do the three women have to go and tell His disciples first? Will Jesus look the same? Is He easy to recognize? Is He upset? What was death like? What will He do when He is seen? What will He say?

Isn't this just like us in times of suffering, sadness, and sorrow? We want to know what God is doing. We ask acute questions.

---

17. Mark Strauss, *A Survey of the New Testament*, 5th *Edition* (Grand Rapids, MI: Zondervan Academic, 2012), 181.

Why is He waiting to appear to us? When will I see Him? How is He relieving my pain?

The abruptness of this ending helps us to feel the way the women felt. We put ourselves in their place. And we learn that even those closest to Jesus had just as many questions as we do now. The only certainty this ending gives is the certainty there will always be uncertainty—and more questions to ask, especially in times of suffering. It confirms what G. K. Chesterton says, "He has permitted the twilight." This keeps us thinking and bringing our questions to the text. We find ourselves on the seashore, staring into the darkness of the night while the waves pound the sand. We're alone with our questions, wondering what He's doing out there.

THE ONLY CERTAINTY WE HAVE IS THAT THERE WILL ALWAYS BE UNCERTAINTY. AND YET WE KNOW THAT GOD IS OUT THERE SOMEWHERE, ALIVE AND WORKING IN THE MYSTERY.

And yet the abrupt ending *confirms* that Jesus is out there… somewhere…on the other side of the tomb. God winks from the unknown spaces and moments of time. We aren't precisely sure where He is. But wherever He is, He is at work. He is alive in the mystery. In the enigmatic world of chaos, God is in Christ Jesus, now reconciling all things to Himself, having beaten the power of death. Though most of our questions cannot be answered, we know He is up to something for our good. He's on the other side of the tomb, solving the problem of evil and suffering—a problem too big and too complex for us to understand right now.

Though we live in a culture that makes us crave certainty, the Scriptures reprogram us to accept uncertainty, especially given life's hardest questions. This is what Mark's ending does. It lets us know that it's par for the course to have deep questions in times of intense sorrow, sadness, and grief. Our imaginations are left to wonder where God is in these moments. Is He here or there? What's He waiting for? When will dawn burst upon us to dispel the twilight?

Silence. Not having the answer *is* the answer...at least for now.

This summons us to have faith. It invites us to take comfort in realizing that *we don't need to have the answer for God to work.* He's out there doing His job as the re-creator of all things. God winks from the unknown. He nods from the mystery. Ultimately, all things will be made right—for the innocent and for those in turmoil; for the marginalized, poor, and sidelined; for His followers and for those who will be His disciples; for you and for me. *All will be well, and every kind of thing will be well.* We *can* be certain of *this.*

The Scriptures wink.

FINAL WORD

When I initially had the idea to write this book, I wondered if it was a fruitful project worth pursuing. I asked myself, "Is this something I could start and carry to the finish line? Should I pitch it to the publisher? Or is it just an idea I can throw around for conversation when I am with other writers and theologians?" I considered the pros, but mostly the cons.

The cons were somewhat daunting. First, this book accepts and even encourages mystery and uncertainty. In our scientific culture, mystery is never enough. Mystery is a problem awaiting a solution. The quicker we solve the mystery, the better off we are. Moreover, who would want to read a book that admits far more uncertainty than answers? In the Christian community, we are accustomed to hearing sermons and reading devotionals that point the way forward with certainty. How would a book that makes room for the twilight fare in this day and age? Would my readers throw the book at the wall? I hoped not.

Second, to make matters more unnerving, I'm writing about suffering. Yikes! Way to ruin the party. Go ahead and talk about your theology of suffering at the next outing you're on and see how that goes over. You're likely to hear, "Hey, let's talk about something a little more uplifting, why don't we?" Many in our culture have forged ahead in health and wealth teaching. Thinking has set sail in that direction. I mused that an examination of suffering might not work so well in light of some of the contemporary teaching of our day, especially when the outcome of such a study doesn't necessarily promise a way out of our suffering here and now.

Third, I was approaching this book using narrative criticism, a hermeneutical technique not generally familiar to most readers. Instead of scrutinizing grammar, getting behind the text using history, or even laying out propositions about theology, I'd be examining story elements to yield theology and ideals. It's a different avenue for exploring the Bible. This could be a plus…but it could also be a negative.

The final checkmark in the negative column was bringing all of this together into one book. There are theological books on suffering. There are hermeneutical textbooks on narrative criticism. There are even books that appreciate the components of mystery and ambiguity in Scripture. But all of these together in one book? To the best of my knowledge, it has never been done before.

All of these possible cons. All of this uncertainty. All of this mystery surrounding this book.

How exciting! What more could I ask for? The unknown was all I needed to begin.

I pray that after having gone through these studies, you appreciate uncertainty. I pray you embrace mystery. I pray that you can admire the story and see God wink. In doing so, I pray that you trust that the Captain of our salvation is leading us through the darkness of the night to our eternal home filled with His light, where the problem of suffering and evil is solved.

ABOUT THE AUTHOR

The Rev. Chris Palmer is a pastor, missionary, theology professor, and Koine Greek scholar who makes God's Word come alive in a unique way. He is also host of the popular podcast *Greek for the Week*.

Chris has travelled to more than forty nations and has helped many congregations grow, flourish, and expand. His desire for missions is to train and educate pastors, encourage congregations, support the vision of the local church, and show the love of God to the culture. He has worked successfully with both traditional churches and the underground, persecuted church.

A member of the teaching faculty at Moody Bible Institute, Chris is also dean of Theos U and Theos Seminary. His Ph.D. studies are in the book of Revelation at the University of Wales, Bangor.

Chris is the author of several books, including *Greek Word Study: 90 Ancient Words That Unlock Scripture*; *Letters from Jesus: Studies from the Seven Churches of Revelation*; and *Strange Scriptures: Deciphering 52 Weird, Bizarre, and Curious Verses from the New*

Testament. His articles have been published by *Charisma, CBN, Crosswalk, The Christian Post,* and more.

You may find Chris online at:

twitter.com/chrispalmer

www.instagram.com/chrispalmer

www.facebook.com/greekfortheweek

www.chrispalmer.me

BIBLIOGRAPHY

The following works have influenced this book and my approach to suffering in the biblical text. I have built upon their ideas, methodologies, and approaches.

Adams, Marilyn McCord. "Horrendous Evils and the Goodness of God," in *The Problem of Evil*, edited by Marilyn McCord Adams and Robert Merrihew Adams (Oxford, UK: Oxford University Press, 1990), 209–221.

The Apostolic Faith (Azusa Street Mission, Los Angeles, CA, 1906–1908).

Augustine of Hippo, *Confessions*, trans. Henry Chadwick (Oxford, UK: Oxford University Press, 1990).

The Bridegroom's Messenger (The Pentecostal Mission, Atlanta, GA, 1907–1941).

Brown, Jeannine K. *The Gospels as Stories: A Narrative Approach to Matthew, Mark, Luke, and John* (Grand Rapids, MI: Baker Academic, 2020).

Carson, D.A. *How Long, O Lord? Reflections on Suffering and Evil, Second Edition* (Grand Rapids, MI: Baker Academic, 2006).

The Church of God Evangel (Church of God, Cleveland, TN, est. 1910).

DC Talk. *Jesus Freaks: Martyrs: Stories of Those Who Stood for Jesus: The Ultimate Jesus Freaks* (Bloomington, MN: Bethany House Publishers, 1999).

De Dietrich, Suzanne. *The Gospel According to St. Matthew* (London, UK: John Knox Press, 1961).

Douglass, Eric. *Interpreting New Testament Narratives: Recovering the Author's Voice*, vol. 169 of the Biblical Interpretation Series (Boston, MA: Brill, 2018).

Eusebius of Caesaria. *Eusebius: Church History, Life of Constantine the Great, and Oration in Praise of Constantine*, ed. Philip Schaff and Henry Wace, trans. Arthur Cushman McGiffert, Volume 1 A. Select Library of the Nicene and Post-Nicene Fathers of the Christian Church, Second Series (New York: NY: Christian Literature Company, 1890).

Lewis, C. S. *A Grief Observed* (New York, NY: Seabury Press, 1976).

London, Daniel DeForest. *Theodicy and Spirituality in the Fourth Gospel: A Girardian Perspective* (New York, NY: Lexington Books/ Fortress Academic Press, 2020).

Morris, Leon. *The Gospel According to Matthew* (Grand Rapids, MI: William B. Eerdman's Publishing Company, 1992).

Pope Francis. "Homily of His Holiness Pope Francis," Vatican Basilica, Vatican City, February 15, 2015, accessed June 16, 2021, vatican.va.

Powell, Mark Allan. *What is Narrative Criticism?* (Minneapolis, MN: Fortress Press, 1990).

Resseguie, James L. *Narrative Criticism of the New Testament: An Introduction* (Grand Rapids, MI: Baker Academic, 2005).

Stevenson, Gregory. *A Slaughtered Lamb: Revelation and the Apocalyptic Response to Evil and Suffering* (Abilene, TX: Abilene Christian University Press, 2013).

Strauss, Mark. *A Survey of the New Testament*, 5th edition (Grand Rapids, MI: Zondervan Academic, 2012).

Thomas, John Christopher. *The Apocalypse: A Literary and Theological Commentary* (Cleveland, TN: CPT Press, 2012).

Warrington, Keith. *Pentecostal Theology: A Theology of Encounter* (New York, NY: T&T Clark, 2008).

Wright, N. T. *John for Everyone: Part 2 Chapter 11–21* (Louisville, KY: Westminster John Knox, 2004).

Welcome to Our House!

We Have a Special Gift for You

It is our privilege and pleasure to share in your love of Christian books. We are committed to bringing you authors and books that feed, challenge, and enrich your faith.

To show our appreciation, we invite you to sign up to receive a specially selected **Reader Appreciation Gift**, with our compliments. Just go to the Web address at the bottom of this page.

God bless you as you seek a deeper walk with Him!

WE HAVE A GIFT FOR YOU. VISIT:

whpub.me/nonfictionthx

WHITAKER
HOUSE